Collage Your Life

BEN LEWIS GILES

THIS is no work of mine.

It lies

It isn't really a gate

you could get peace and quiet.

247

Collage Your Life

Techniques, Prompts, and Inspiration for

CREATIVE SELF-EXPRESSION and VISUAL STORYTELLING

MELANIE MOWINSKI

Storey Publishing

The mission of Storey Publishing is to serve our customers by
publishing practical information that encourages
personal independence in harmony with the environment.

EDITED BY Liz Bevilacqua and Mia Lumsden
ART DIRECTION AND BOOK DESIGN BY Carolyn Eckert
TEXT PRODUCTION BY Liseann Karandisecky and
Jennifer Jepson Smith
INDEXED BY Christine R. Lindemer, Boston Road
Communications

COVER AND INTERIOR PHOTOGRAPHY BY Mars Vilaubi © Storey
Publishing, LLC
ADDITIONAL COVER PHOTOGRAPHY BY © Amy Duncan/studio four
corners, *Roy*, mixed media collage, back m.r.; © Ben Lewis Giles
@ Début Art, inside front; © Evita Tezeno, back b.r.; courtesy of
Kaci Smith, back t.r.
ADDITIONAL INTERIOR PHOTOGRAPHY BY © 2016 Andrés
Charbonnier Aunchayna, *Rainy Nights* – Mixed Media Collage,
34; © 2020 Ginger Sedlarova, 168; courtesy of Aaron Gordon,
140, 142; Adam Hutcheson, 143; © Alma Larroca, 15, 82; © Amy
Duncan/studio four corners, *The Lepidopterist*, work in progress, 4;
© Amy Duncan/studio four corners, *Roy*, mixed media collage, 151;
© Anthony Zinonos, 33 b.; 107; © Argyle Plaids, 18 r.; © Ben Lewis
Giles, 2; © Ben Lewis Giles @ Début Art, ii, vi; © Billy Renkl, 35 t., 111;
© Brandon Brewer, 137; © Brenda Rose, *Canoe*, 155; © Brenda
Rose, *Mountain Goat*, 36 t.; Charlota Blunarova/Unsplash, 44;
© Charlotte D'Aigle, *Talisman*, acrylic/paper collage on board,
12" × 9", 179 l.; © Ciara Phelan, viii; © Colin Johnson Illustration, 86;
© Connor "Phib" Dainty, 19; © connylehmannART/www.aquarelle
-connylehmann.com, 123; © Craig Upson, 84 r.; courtesy of e bond,
175; © Emanuele Crovetto, 41; © Emily Marbach, 113; © Erica K.
Smith, 179 r.; © Erin McCluskey Wheeler, *Adventitious II*, 2021,
painted paper, photographs, and cyanotypes mounted on wood,
23; © Evita Tezeno, 118–121; FeMail Collage postcards from the mail
art collection by Karen Arp-Sandel, 161; © Gabriela Szulman, 36 b.;
© Guillaume Chiron, *Le col du Julie*, Collage, 16.5 × 31 cm 2014,
171 l.; © Heather Matthew, 131; © Heather Polk, *Tropical Delight*,
collage on mixed media paper, 14" × 11", 2019, 101; © instagram.
com/ilonkacollages, 95; © Isabel Espanol, 85 l.; © Ivaldo Ferreira,
Strong girl, play and record, 2021, 133; © Jacinta Bunnell, 13; © Jack
Felice, 180 r.; © Johanna Goodman, *The Catalogue of Imaginary
Beings, Plate No. 88*, 181 r.; © Johanna Goodman, *The Catalogue of
Imaginary Beings, Plate No. 392*, 157; © Julia Nala, 180 l.; courtesy
of Kaci Smith, 28, 42, 96, 98, 99; © Karen Lynch, Leaf and Petal
Design, 40; © Kike Congrains, 146; © Klawe Rzeczy, photographs
from Library of Congress, 20, 38, 39; © Laura Didyk, 145, 176, 177;
© Laura Weiler, photos sourced from *National Geographic*, 129,
178; © Linden Eller, *Go Again Home, Can't You*, mixed media,
16" × 12", 2019, 162; © Linden Eller, *Honey*, collage on felt, 14 × 14",
2017, 21 t.r.; © Maddalena Notardonato, *Audiocasetta*, 84 l.;
© Melanie Mowinski, 112, 134; © Michelle Dow, incorporating art by
Cindy Sherman from *Tate Etc* magazine, 85 r.; © Natalie Nelson,
29; © Pamela Towns, 102; © Patricia Doucet, 117; © Rosemary
Rae, *Issue*, 2019, 10; © Roy Gentes, 1 t.; © Ruby Silvious, used with
permission of the artist, 115; © Samantha Malay, *Autumn Travel #7*
collage: vintage fabric, Japanese cookie packaging, beeswax;
4.25" × 5.5", 2019, 27; © Sarah Jarrett, *Identity Unknown*, 181 l.;
© Sarah Jarrett, *Tree of Bones*, 153; shraga kopstein/Unsplash,
56; © Simon Blake, original collage, 2017, 37; © Suzi Banks Baum,
104–105; Thomas Renaud/Unsplash, 25; © Vadim Solovyev, digital
artist, 159
GRAPHICS BY Ilona Sherratt © Storey Publishing, LLC, 65, 185, 191, 192
LETTERS BY patricia m/Flickr/CC BY-SA, 5, 43, 87, 183

Storey books are available at special discounts when purchased in
bulk for premiums and sales promotions as well as for fund-raising
or educational use. Special editions or book excerpts can also be
created to specification. For details, please call 800-827-8673, or
send an email to sales@storey.com.

Storey Publishing
210 MASS MoCA Way
North Adams, MA 01247
storey.com

Printed in the United States by Versa Press
10 9 8 7 6 5 4 3 2 1

Practice
TAKES
Practice

BEN LEWIS GILES

Contents

Build Your Materials

A good toolbox contains more than objects. Explore general tools and materials, plus the building blocks of design and composition, to get started.

Develop Your Techniques

Collage extends beyond the actions of cutting and pasting. Learn basic collage methods plus how to mix other mediums into your collection of techniques.

55 Prompts to Jump-Start Your Practice

The heart of this book! Dive into this chapter for prompts and inspiration to nurture and develop your own voice.

Create the Container

Learn how to construct different kinds of handmade books to showcase your collages.

CIARA PHELAN

What Do You Love?

What do you collect and save?
What materials speak to you?

Maybe you pick up feathers when you walk in the woods, paint chips at the hardware store, quotes from your favorite writers or influencers, images of circles, vintage boxes, and magazines, you know what I mean. Those pieces of ephemera that just have to be in your life.

Perhaps you have piles of children's drawings and paintings, or birthday cards from your youth. Maybe they live in file folders or in a box. Possibly you have random scraps of things all over your house that you have always wanted to put together somehow. Maybe you want to use items (such as ticket stubs) to document significant occasions. Or as a chronicle of a momentous time in your life, or even just the days' events.

Let the ephemera you collect and love guide you to create. Doing so just might lead you to your own visual style. You might discover you like bold imagery on a muted background, or three dimensions paired with flat stylized shapes. You may like to include feathers or found objects in compositions, or decide that you only want to use the color green. Whatever it is, it is **YOU**.

I have categorized folders of papers from various periods of my life containing old letters, my childhood artwork, newspaper clippings, and more. And then there are the piles of magazine cutouts, file folder boxes of various categories, and boxes of groovy magazines and papers for random exploration. When I want to create a collage, looking through my complete collection of papers is overwhelming. Sometimes I choose a few pieces of paper from each of these collections at random as a starting point. Other times I begin with a prompt and search my collections for a specified amount of time. The point is just to start.

What you make doesn't matter.
All that matters is that you make something.

Maybe you are new to collage- and art-making and the thought of making something scares you. You are in the right place. Go where the fear takes you. And make something.

Maybe you are a seasoned collage- and art-making person but are looking for inspiration or a new direction. You are in the right place. Go where the open door leads you. And make something.

If you can make something and not care about it or be attached to it, even better. (Yes, this is hard!) Commit to making and being okay with "bad" art. When you show up consistently, put your judge in silent mode, and make something, the faucet of inspiration is more likely to turn on. Connections will become easier, and you will take more and more risks. Sometimes you will make something you like. Sometimes you won't. Like any kind of practice, you have to cultivate it to make it grow while also finding your peace with uncertainty and those compositions you don't like.

This book will guide you! We begin with a chapter that will help you develop a set of skills over time. This leads us into a chapter that will teach you techniques for turning the items you collect into collage form.

BEN LEWIS GILES

We will also explore the challenges of maintaining an art practice, as well as tips and tricks for overcoming those challenges. My goal is to encourage you along your creative path by offering suggestions for how to find ideas wherever you are in the world, in your life, and in your making journey.

Throughout the book there are sample collages, examples from outside artists, and prompts—but remember all of those are simply ideas. Use this book to help you discover what you love to make.

To get us started, let's think about the myriad ways to weave your collections into a collage practice. Some may draw on a specific medium and technique, others may derive from the elements and principles of design, narrative, momentous moments, and more. Perhaps you want to use collage in your journal as a way to organize your ephemera. Or maybe you've read about commonplace books—one of the earliest forms of scrapbooking—and you want to make your own as a way to collect all these things you love. As you might imagine, the list is endless. Our hope is that you will use this book as a springboard to your own making. We won't cover everything in these pages, but we will get you started. In Chapter 3, some of the prompts and techniques will help you explore different ways of working. Take a dip into that chapter, and let yourself be inspired.

I make a letterpress card that says "Practice Takes Practice." Anyone who commits to daily exercise, yoga, making, or anything that involves skill knows this to be true. Developing a practice takes commitment, which means regular, focused attention on continual skill refinement. It's never a perfect process. There will be ups and downs and setbacks, as well as "Aha!" moments and breakthroughs. This book is designed to help you establish an art practice that reflects what you love through the materials and techniques you use, and the projects, prompts, and sources of inspiration you choose.

Come along with me; I'll give you pep talks and encouragement along the way. You can do this.

All it takes is practice.

chapter **1**

AMY DUNCAN

Build Your Materials

**VERY ARTIST** develops their box of tools over time. Most collage artists begin with a pair of scissors, some glue, and a stack of paper. Other tools get added when needed. As you dive deeper into the collage process, you might want a tool for cutting fine lines and perfect circles or maybe something to smooth out air bubbles on glued paper. You'll discover pretty quickly that collage-making can involve as many or as few tools as you like. However, a good toolbox contains more than objects. Let's explore.

General Tools

The following tools are those that I think every collage artist should have in their toolbox, since you'll use them constantly.

SCISSORS. There are scissors for every kind of cutting job. Large ones for big, bold, rough cuts and tiny ones for small pieces of paper or details—plus several in between. You can find scissors with wavy, zigzag, or other kinds of patterns in most scrapbooking supply stores. Add scissors to your tool collection as your work dictates.

OTHER CUTTING TOOLS. Keep a variety of craft knives (I like X-Acto knives and #11 blades) ready for detail cuts, among other kinds of cutting work. An X-Acto knife with a mini-flashlight near the tip helps you to see the detail work, while Olfa brand snap-off blade utility knives work well for cutting substrates (or base layers) and thicker materials. Use anything that can help systemize and ease your cutting, including circle cutters and punches. Always keep extra blades on hand, too. Accidents are more likely to happen with dull blades.

CUTTING MAT. All cutting should be done on a self-healing cutting mat, if possible. Use a large one as a placemat on your worktable, plus have a few smaller cutting mats ready to slip into place as needed. Use them not only to protect your work surface, but also as measuring devices. Most come with grid lines, which you can use to help you make both rough and precision cuts. In a pinch, you can substitute cardboard from any kind of box for a cutting mat. The cardboard backing on pads of newsprint, drawing, and other kinds of paper is perfect for this.

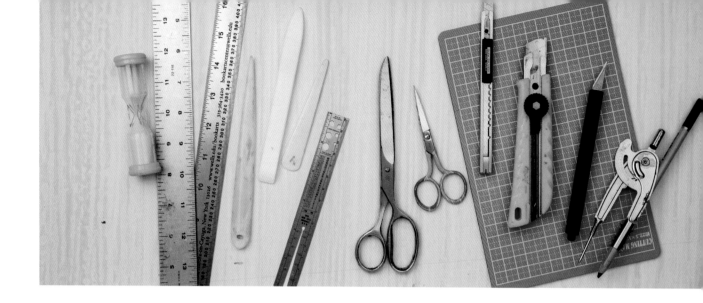

RULERS. Rulers of all lengths are useful. Always keep a short (6-inch) and a long (18-inch) ruler in your toolbox. In addition, 12-, 24-, and 36-inch rulers can be helpful. Choose rulers that have centimeters and inches, because sometimes centimeters are easier to work with. When you're cutting with a craft knife, it's best to use a metal or metal-edged ruler, since plastic and wood can get nicked by the blade, ruining the ruler for drawing straight lines. If your metal ruler has a cork bottom, for precision cutting it's better to flip that faceup so your blade doesn't slip underneath the ruler.

TIMER. Using a timer challenges you to complete your work in a designated amount of time. This can be useful when you don't have a lot of time to work and you need to be mindful. It also can be especially valuable if you struggle to make creative decisions. A timer can be analog or digital. If you are trying to limit screen time, definitely get yourself an analog timer.

BONE FOLDERS. Bone folders (shown above, to the right of the long rulers) are used by bookbinders to score and crease folds. Collage artists use bone folders to smooth out paper and banish air bubbles. Although these tools were originally made from bone, the name *bone folder* is misleading because now many are made from plastic, horn, and Teflon. While Teflon folders are more expensive than bone or plastic folders, they perform the best. Glue never sticks to Teflon folders, they don't mar the paper, and the action is very smooth when you use them to burnish, smooth out air bubbles, or work to commit your adhesive. Bone folders come in a variety of shapes and sizes.

COMPASS. Drafting compasses let you make circles easily. Maybe you want to mix mediums and create outlines for a circle to paint or you need to cut out a circle—if circle perfection appeals to you, keep a compass in your toolbox.

BRUSHES are important for applying both paint and adhesive. Never use the same brush for both mediums, though. Stiffer brushes work well for most glues, and short brushes work well for general adhesive, but you should have a variety of brush sizes to use depending on the job. For painting, sable brushes are the best. For stenciling, choose brushes with short, firmly packed bristles. If you really dive into stenciling, get a few brushes in varying widths. Keep some water brush pens on hand, too (I like Niji).

MARKERS, PENS, AND PENCILS come in a wide range of mediums, tips, colors, and more. Choose what you love.

OTHER TOOLS

In addition to the above-mentioned tools, which you'll use frequently, here are several items that you'll probably find helpful but most likely won't use every time you sit down to make a collage.

TEMPLATES such as circles, arrows, and boxes are readily available in a range of sizes and are a great alternative to a compass.

VERSA-TOOL is a type of woodburning tool with knife attachments. You plug in the tool to heat the blade, making it easy to cut out stencils from Mylar and other plastic-like stenciling materials. When you use a Versa-Tool you'll need a piece of glass for your cutting surface so you don't burn a hole in your cutting mat.

STENCILS can be purchased or you can make your own from transparencies, stencil film, or thin cardboard. You can even use shapes from magazines, found objects, and more as stencils.

STAMPS AND STAMP PADS can be used to add predesigned generic imagery and text to your collage. Pair the stamps with a dye or with a pigment-based stamp pad, which tends to be water-resistant and lightfast. You can also carve your own stamps from corks, erasers, and other materials, including E-Z-Cut printing blocks.

Materials

Materials can range from paper you collect throughout your day or find in your recycling box to high-end fancy papers, vintage magazines, and more. What kinds of papers call to you?

SUBSTRATES

A substrate is the base layer for any collage and can range from medium-heavy papers such as Bristol board and printmaking papers to cardboard, Davey board, or other materials. Choose a substrate to support the mediums you will be using to create your collage. If you intend to use only paper, you'll likely be fine with a heavy paper substrate. The more layers, materials, and mediums you use in your collage, the stronger the substrate you'll need. As you experiment, you may want to try using canvas panels, hardboard or plywood, or even painting panels as substrates. Really, everything is fair game. Experiment and test whenever in doubt. Here are some of the most common substrates.

MEDIUM- TO HEAVYWEIGHT PAPERS are what most of the collages in this book were built on. Use found or purchased papers—aim for paper weight that is 80 lb. or heavier. Bristol board, manila envelopes, some magazine covers, index cards, card stock, printmaking papers, and water-color papers are all good options for medium- or heavyweight paper.

CARDBOARD can be found everywhere, especially in things that might otherwise end up in your recycling bin. Corrugated cardboard works especially well for book covers.

DAVEY BOARD comes in a variety of thicknesses and is used primarily by bookbinders. It works well as a substrate for heavier mediums.

MAT BOARD also comes in a variety of thicknesses. Sometimes offcuts are available from framing stores for a good deal.

Substrates come in a variety of colors, textures, and thicknesses. Here are just a few options: A) mat board; B) cardboard; C) found cardboard; D) plywood; E) canvas board; F) newsprint; G) card stock; H) manila file folder; I) Davey board; J) various printmaking and watercolor papers; and K) date book.

Did You Know?

Weight is the term that describes the thickness of paper. Regular writing papers, or text-weight papers, can come in weights of 24 lb., 28 lb., 32 lb., and 44 lb., while medium- to heavy-weight papers can come in weights of 80 lb., 100 lb., and 130 lb. and are often called cover-weight paper or card stock. The number is determined by the "basis weight" of 500 sheets, or a ream, of that type of paper in its original, uncut form.

APRIL 23

Let the collector in you shine!

PAPERS

Gathering papers for collage-making can be just as much fun as making the collages. Much of it starts with you and what your interests are. This is where your collections of ephemera, papers, notes, and other things come in handy. You can also make rules for yourself, such as you aren't allowed to purchase any papers; they all must be found. Or maybe you only use *National Geographic* magazines. Whatever you decide, let your **YOU** shine.

In addition to being classified by weight, paper can also be classified by surface, usage, or even brightness and opacity. Try to become familiar with paper terms and categories so you will have a better idea of which paper will be best for the job you want it to do. Below are some examples of the many kinds of paper you can use.

TRANSPARENT PAPERS: sewing patterns, some handmade papers, tracing paper, and tissue paper.

COLORED PAPERS: construction paper, colored pages from magazines, Color-aid paper, and found papers. Organize them by color so they're ready when needed.

PASTE PAPER AND OTHER PAINTED PAPERS: Paint papers yourself using pigmented paste, acrylics, watercolors, or inks.

HANDMADE PAPERS: all kinds of weights, patterns, and thicknesses. Dive in and explore.

MAGAZINE PAPERS: magazines, catalogs, and brochures. You never know where you will find inspiration.

VINTAGE PAPERS: postcards, magazines, letters, and drawings from kids (either from your own childhood or, if you have kids, your children's drawings)

TEXT PAPERS: headlines, paragraphs, and words on paper. Cut out text that speaks to you, and keep your cutouts in an envelope or file for future use.

FOUND PAPERS: receipts from the post office (or heck, from anywhere), ticket stubs, insides of security envelopes. Paper waits for you everywhere.

WASTE PAPERS: old telephone books, catalogs, magazines. All of these can become waste papers. One of the really great things about using a multi-page document is when you flip the page, you have a new work surface.

OTHER MATERIALS

Throughout this book, we will explore a variety of collage-making techniques, ranging from how to apply adhesives and use a bone folder to incorporating mixed mediums into your compositions. You will use many of the materials below in your collages.

WASHI TAPE is tape made from Japanese rice paper. It is similar to masking tape but is available in a variety of widths, textures, patterns, and colors.

GESSO is a primer for canvas that is typically used to make a surface less porous. In this book we hack gesso and use it instead as a medium for stenciling, masking, and neutralizing papers. Gesso is usually white but also comes in black. Both create an opaque surface when dry.

PACKING TAPE can be used for encapsulating found objects, joining papers together, and making transfers—a process by which you lift the ink off a photocopy or a magazine sheet and transfer it to another surface (see page 60).

PAINTING MEDIUMS of all kinds exist in the world. You'll want to choose water-based paints such as watercolor, gouache, or acrylic paints, as well as acrylic and India inks. Paint quality varies from brand to brand. Better quality paints have more pigment in them, which results in richer colors. Invest in the best you can afford.

PHOTOCOPIES of patterned papers, images from magazines, and things such as your hands, found objects, and commercial packaging can be used as is or with packing tape to make a transfer. Photocopiers and printers use different kinds of inks and toners. Some work with some transfers, others don't. When in doubt, try it out.

OTHER EPHEMERA. Okay, so really—anything can be used. String. Yarn. Feathers. Pieces of metal. Shells. Netting. Sticks. Leaves. Fabric. Felt. Plastic. If it inspires you somehow, use it.

If it inspires you somehow, use it.

ALMA LARROCA

ADHESIVES

Not all adhesives are the same, and you'll want to make sure you choose the right one so that your work will stick. The heavier the materials you're using, the stronger the adhesive you'll need. The lighter the materials, the lighter the adhesive.

Some adhesives are synthetic, others are organic. Pastes are starch-based, and *glue* is a general term that encompasses all other adhesives, some of which contain animal products and some of which are synthetic. If you are a strict vegan, you'll want to examine your adhesives to make sure you are using a synthetic adhesive or a paste. Choose adhesives that are acid-free and archival. They hold up longer and result in sturdier, longer-lasting work.

POLYVINYL ACETATE (PVA) is an all-purpose white synthetic adhesive and my go-to adhesive for heavier papers and boards. I use Jade 403, an archival bookbinding adhesive. Not all white adhesives are acid-free and archival. Be sure to read the labels.

GLUE STICKS are a great adhesive to use for thin materials and on-the-go art-making. Not all glue sticks are alike, though. Choose one that is permanent and acid-free. I keep a UHU Stic brand glue stick in my art kit at all times. When it comes to glue sticks, the word *glue* is a misnomer, as these handy adhesives tend to be made from starches so are really paste.

ACRYLIC MEDIUMS come in all kinds of finishes. A glossy finish will be shiny, while a matte finish will be flat. Both matte and gloss mediums work for thin papers such as sewing patterns and tissue papers. They can be used to glue, layer, or add a finishing touch.

PASTES are made from various powdered starches such as wheat and rice. Some of these powders can be mixed in cold water to create a paste-like consistency, while others need to be cooked on a stovetop. The benefits of pastes include that they dry more slowly than glues, dry clear, and are all natural.

MOUNTING ADHESIVES are thin adhesive films that function like double-stick tape. The adhesive is protected with a removable release paper. Mounting adhesives are a great option for delicate cutouts. Apply the adhesive film first, burnish in place, and cut out your image. When you're ready, strip off the release paper and adhere to your collage. Gudy 870 (often called Gudy O) is my favorite mounting adhesive, but I also keep a couple of rolls of 3M 415 double-stick tape in varying thicknesses in my art kit. All of these adhesives are acid-free and do not discolor with age.

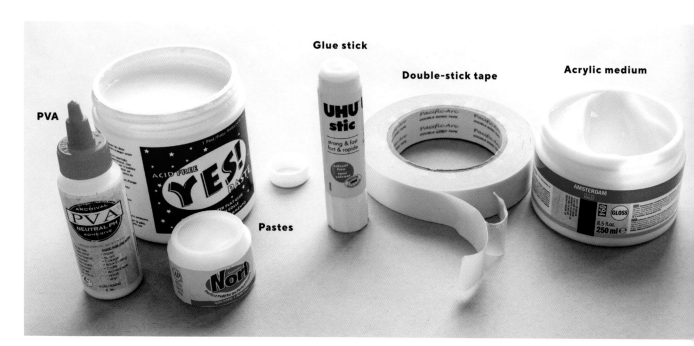

PVA · Glue stick · Double-stick tape · Acrylic medium · Pastes

Building Blocks of Design

Once you have the physical objects in your toolbox, it's time to start thinking about the conceptual tools that you'll use to create your collages. You may already be familiar with some elements of art and principles of design, the concepts that direct artists toward composition, construction, and more. As you progress in your collage-making, these guidelines can support your decision-making. For example, pair flat shapes with forms that appear three-dimensional to create contrast and emphasize a particular concept or idea.

Use the elements of art to create your work. Use the principles of design to guide *how* you use the elements and to help you organize compositions. Some of the following concepts will find their way into the prompts and inspirations in Chapter 3. Look for them as you read.

ELEMENTS

ARGYLE PLAIDS

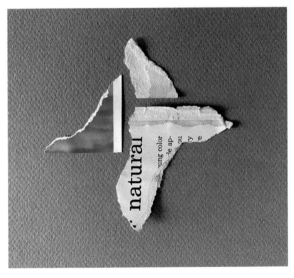

LINE. A long, narrow mark; an outlined edge; or a series of points or dots that occur in a straight progression.

SPACE. This element creates depth or three dimensions using perspective, overlap, size, gradation, or value.

The term *space* also refers to how you use the area within the picture plane. As a collage artist, the difference between positive and negative space can become a big part of your practice: Positive space is the object you are cutting out, and the remaining paper (or the space around the object) is negative space.

FORM

SHAPE

SHAPE and **FORM.** Both refer to a visible item or contour.
A shape is flat, like a silhouette. A form has depth and shading.

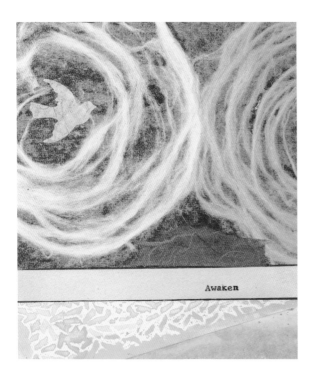

TEXTURE. The way a surface appears to feel and the way a surface actually feels. Try incorporating both kinds of texture into your collage. Some examples of texture include rough, smooth, fuzzy, sharp, soft, hard, and wet.

VALUE. The lightness or darkness of a color.

COLOR. The visible characteristic produced when light strikes an object and the wavelengths are reflected back to the eye. Often described in terms of hue, value, and intensity, color is everywhere. You have your personal favorites, as well as those you gravitate toward in your artwork. Color evokes mood and attaches itself to emotion. For example, warm colors such as red, orange, and yellow tend to be associated with happiness or energy, while cool colors such as purple, blue, and green tend to be associated with sadness or quiet. Use these associations to express in your work what you are feeling as you create.

Color Basics
Most color theory hinges on three words: **HUE**, **VALUE**, and **INTENSITY**.

HUE is the name of a particular color.

VALUE describes how light or dark a color is.

INTENSITY (OR SATURATION) describes the pureness of a color, which our brain interprets as how bright or dull the color is. Adding black to a pure color produces a *shade*. Adding white to a pure color produces a *tint*. Adding gray to a pure color produces a *tone*.

ERIN McCLUSKEY WHEELER

Color Basics *continued*

Colors are grouped in the following ways:

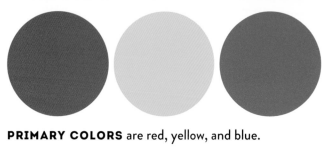

PRIMARY COLORS are red, yellow, and blue.

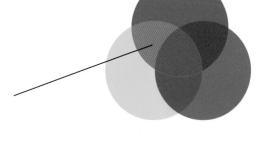

SECONDARY COLORS are orange, green, and purple.
They are created by mixing two primary colors together.

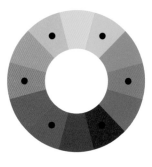

TERTIARY COLORS are created by mixing a secondary color with its neighboring primary color;
red-orange; yellow-orange; yellow-green; blue-green; blue-purple; and red-purple.

THOMAS RENAUD

Color Basics *continued*

What colors go best together depends on what kind of look or feeling you're trying to evoke or express. The following color combinations can get you started:

COMPLEMENTARY COLORS are opposite each other on the color wheel. When they are paired together, compositions appear to vibrate.

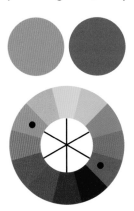

SPLIT COMPLEMENTARY combinations include any color on the color wheel plus the two colors that border its complement.

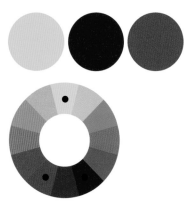

SAMANTHA MALAY

ANALOGOUS COLORS are adjacent on the color wheel. These combinations include one primary, one secondary, and one tertiary color.

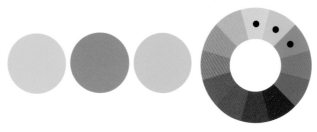

Color Basics *continued*

KACI SMITH

TRIADIC combinations include any three colors that are evenly spaced on the color wheel.

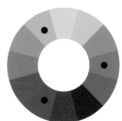

TETRADIC/DOUBLE-COMPLEMENTARY combinations include complementary pairs. (For best results, choose one of the four complementary pairs to dominate in your piece.)

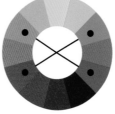

NATALIE NELSON

COOL COLORS, such as blues, blue-greens, blue-purple, and grays, tend to be calming and recede in a composition.

WARM COLORS, such as reds, oranges, yellows, browns, and tans, tend to be stimulating and advance in a composition.

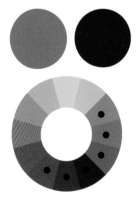

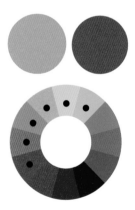

MONOCHROMATIC COLOR combinations rely on tints, tones, and shades of a single hue.

PRINCIPLES

BALANCE. The impression of equilibrium in a composition. Balance can be related to the overall compositional structure (such as symmetrical, asymmetrical, or radial) or to various elements and principles (such as shape, size, and value).

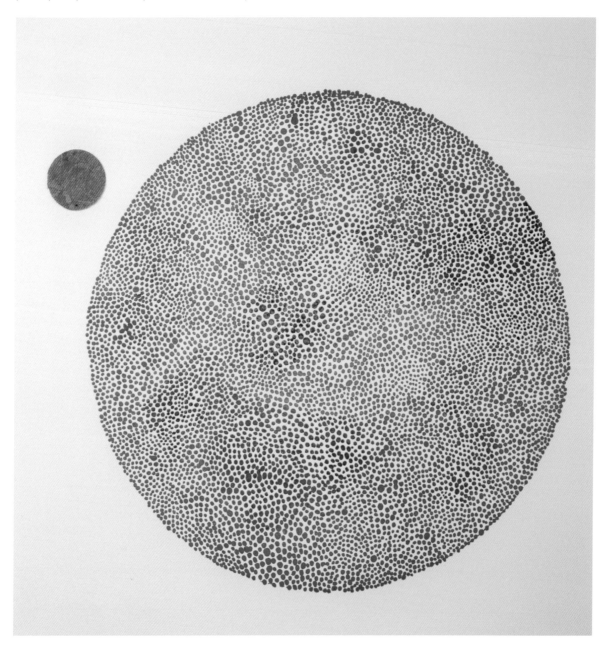

EMPHASIS. The act of making a specific element stand out. Often the emphasis is linked to the composition's focal point or center of interest. The emphasized object or area, however, doesn't have to be in the center to be the focal point.

MOVEMENT/RHYTHM. An eye-path for the observer to follow through the art-work, sometimes created by repeated use of a line, color scheme, shape, or other element.

ANTHONY ZINONOS

PATTERN. A recurring design element. It can be exact or varied. A pattern creates rhythm and a visual beat.

BILLY RENKL

UNITY. The use of colors, shapes, or textures to tie parts of a composition into a cohesive whole.

CONTRAST. Dramatic differences between the components of an image. The contrast can be in shape, size, scale, color, value, or another element.

REPETITION. The reuse of a single object or shape within the composition. Often repetition is used to create movement or to emphasize a particular component.

VARIETY. The use of visually dissimilar elements or objects in a composition. The variety can relate to the position of an element within a composition, the types of objects used, or the conceptual ideas conveyed in the composition.

PROPORTION. The size and scale of elements within a composition. Often proportion is used to create unexpected relationships.

Composition

Composition is the overall layout of your collage or how you put your artwork together. You will use the elements and principles described in Building Blocks of Design (pages 18–37) to organize your papers into a composition. A focal point (or sometimes the lack of a focal point) is the key element in a composition.

What draws the eye in to the piece of art? Is it the placement of one or more objects? Perhaps it's a high contrast between two objects. Maybe you use lines and other elements to call attention directly or indirectly to the focal point. Or maybe there is something so unusual in your collage that the eye automatically looks at it. Ultimately, you want to choose a focal point that draws the eye in and then allows the eye to move through the composition in an interesting way.

Whatever you decide your focal point will be, resist the urge to place it in the center of your composition—try other options before that. Move and shuffle papers. You may be surprised that shifting your focal point to the left or right of center makes all the difference. Before committing to a layout by gluing items in place, try looking at centered, off-centered, circular, cross, or radial patterns and then decide what works best. Often the strongest compositions use a technique called the law of thirds, a way of dividing up the compositional plane into nine blocks with four different axes (plural of axis). The center of interest is placed at an intersection of two of the axes, which is off-center (shown here with red dots).

You may also find that using an odd number of primary objects in a composition works better than an even number of primary objects. When you're beginning, try playing with the number three. There is balance in its imbalance.

In addition, resist putting everything and the kitchen sink into your composition. Fewer items are often better than more items. Always think about how the overall image appears—more items can dilute the power of your focal point.

Background elements

Midground elements

Foreground elements

KAREN LYNCH

EMANUELE
CROVETTO

Even after learning the principles and elements of design, many beginning collage students struggle to create a cohesive composition. The work ends up looking like a vision board or a collection of images that lack visual unity. There is nothing wrong with this. But . . . sometimes you want a unified composition. To get there, remember to create a focal point and consider what you want to emphasize (either compositionally or conceptually), but also start thinking about foreground, midground, and background. Experiment with overlapping objects instead of placing them side by side. Layering paper can suggest depth, space, and more.

Background elements in your composition are perceived as farthest from the viewer. Use smaller, cool-toned objects to help establish the background. Foreground elements are perceived as closest to the viewer. Size and scale help indicate to the viewer that something is in the foreground. Large, bright, warm-colored objects tend to have more detail and come forward, directing the viewer through the composition. Midground elements in the composition are between the foreground and background. Objects in the midground and background tend to be overlapped by objects in the foreground.

chapter **2**

KACI SMITH

Develop Your Techniques

**HE WORD** *collage* comes from the Old French *coller,* meaning "to glue." Collage is created from the actions of cutting to remove and pasting to add. You must have both. This double action can lead to double meanings and double entendres. For example, if you cut a human figure in half and then add bandage-like shapes linking it together, you are simultaneously showing its split and connection. As you cut and paste, explore how you play with these actions.

The techniques in this chapter will become the foundation of your collage practice. As when learning any new skill, you'll need to experiment to find out what works best for you. You'll make mistakes, discover things you hate (and love!), and question what the heck you are doing. That's all normal. There may also be times when you resist; even if you don't want to resist, you somehow still may. That, too, is normal. Eventually, as you begin to master these techniques, they can lead you in the direction of more experimental and mixed-media approaches.

Collage Building

You can build a collage through planning, intuition, or a combination of both. Try out both paths to see what works for you. Most likely you will flip back and forth between the two processes. Before you start building your collages, though, it's important to familiarize yourself with adhesives.

CHARLOTA BLUNAROVA

Basic Adhesive Techniques and Tips

When making a collage that you want to remain intact for a while, you need to choose the right adhesive and ensure that you apply it in a way that guarantees that it will adhere.

- Test different adhesives. How does each one work with different papers? Often seeing this for yourself helps you decide which glue to use.

- Make sure there is an even coating of glue on the entire back of whatever paper or item you are gluing down. Use waste paper underneath to ensure that you really get all the way to the edge.

- Use a bone folder to smooth out the paper onto the collage. This ensures proper adhesion and removes air bubbles.

- When using a brush with any kind of adhesive, wash the brush as soon as you are finished. Dried PVA can render a brush useless. If you forget to wash the brush right away, try soaking it in water for a few days as soon as you remember. Results will vary.

Once you have played around with the following basic adhesive techniques, apply them to the collage-making process.

RADIANT STAR

One way to think about gluing is to think of a radiant star. Place the paper that you want to glue down on top of your waste paper, with the wrong side up. Starting in the center of the paper and moving outward, apply glue with your brush. Try to avoid getting glue on the side of the paper that will eventually face up. By moving from the inside out, you avoid dragging glue underneath the paper, which could happen if you reversed the gluing direction. Use this same technique when working with a glue stick or any other form of adhesive.

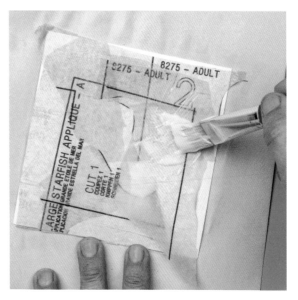

DETAIL WORK

Intricate shapes and images will adhere better if you use a mounting adhesive such as Gudy O (see page 17). Roughly cut the shape you want to adhere close to its edge, then place the wrong side of the shape on the Gudy O. Use a bone folder to burnish the shape to the adhesive release paper. Carefully cut out your intricate shape, then remove the release paper. Position the shape where you want it to stick, and rub with a bone folder to activate the adhesive.

PAINTING WITH ADHESIVE

This technique is best used with acrylic mediums such as Mod Podge, which dries clear. (Some acrylic mediums dry with a glossy finish, while others dry with a matte finish. Choose your favorite!) Brush a layer of medium onto your substrate, add the paper you want to adhere, then brush another layer of medium over the paper. Continue in this manner until you've covered the entire surface. This process will seal and protect the image.

Preplan

Begin a preplanned collage by sorting through papers and choosing ones that inspire you. As you sort and search, use your intuition. As you get more practiced, be intentional by choosing a particular color scheme, a specific focal point, or another idea to help direct your process. Once you've selected images, play. Trust yourself. Trust the process.

TOOLS AND MATERIALS

- **Collage papers**
- **Scissors or craft knife and cutting mat**
- **Sturdy board or paper for building your collage**
- **Adhesive of choice**
- **Brush**
- **Waste paper**

1 Begin by creating a composition. Lay out papers and images in front of you to spark inspiration. Maybe you know your focal point or your background already. Great. Try out different arrangements and compositions. Pair your focal point with different backgrounds. Try different added elements. Consider eye direction and overall flow of the work. Layer papers to create overlaps to suggest a foreground, midground, and background. Work toward creating a pleasing composition.

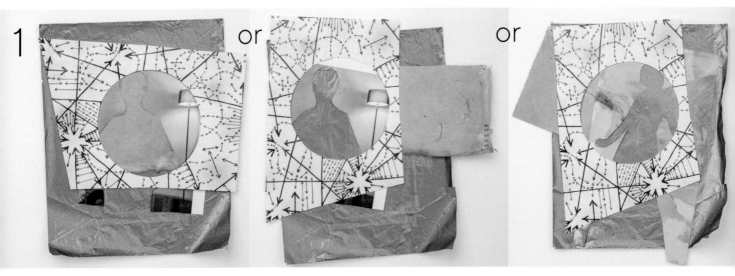

1   or   or

2   Once you are satisfied with your arrangement, commit the plan to memory, do a quick sketch, or snap a picture to remind yourself what goes where.

3   Prepare your substrate by cutting the material to the appropriate size. Your collage can go all the way to the edge of your paper, or you can build in a border around the edge of your composition. For example, maybe you decide to use 11" × 14" paper but your collages are always 9" × 12" centered within the sheet. Try that layout, but also experiment with other ways of filling the page.

4   Build your collage starting from the background (A) and working toward the foreground (B). Use the radiant star gluing technique (page 46) and your adhesive of choice.

5   Once your collage layers are glued in place, you may decide to add other mediums to it or call it complete.

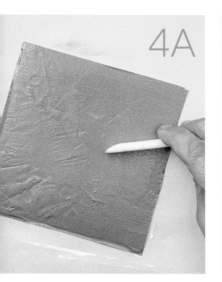

Layer as You Go

This type of collage leaves a lot to chance—which is part of the fun! You'll begin in a similar fashion as you did with a preplanned collage: Gather papers and images that you like. But that's where the similarities end. Now, tap into that intuition!

- **Collage papers**
- **Sturdy board or paper for building your collage**
- **Scissors or craft knife and cutting mat**
- **Adhesive of choice**
- **Brush**
- **Waste paper**

1 Determine your substrate material(s) and size. Cut and prepare your substrate.

2 Glue papers to the substrate for the background. Remember the role that overlapping plays in collage. Some of what you glue for the background will not be seen once you add layers.

3 Examine the background, then consider what kind of additional imagery might lead you to your foreground. Maybe you want your focal point to be in the midground, partially hidden by something in the foreground. Try things out.

4 Add elements in the foreground.

PRO TIP

Don't like something? Glue over it! Or add some gesso or another medium.

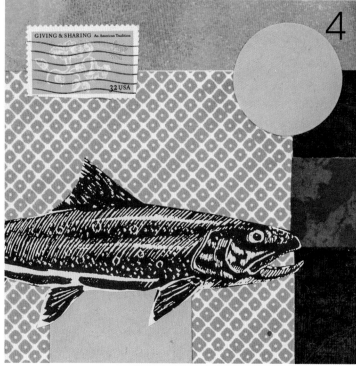

Painting with Papers

This collage technique is similar to the layer-as-you-go technique in the sense that you aren't fully planning out every move ahead of time. But it's different in the sense that you are using paper as paint. As you look through magazines, catalogs, and brochures, start to see how large blocks of gorgeous color are everywhere. Cut out just that, the colors. Look for different values, textures, and patterns, and then group similar ones together. If you enjoy painting, you can "paint" papers using paint, ink, or pigmented paste and use those in your collages as well.

TOOLS AND MATERIALS

- **Matte medium or soft gel medium**
- **Brush**
- **Collage papers**
- **Waste paper**
- **Sturdy board or paper for building your "painting"**
- **Source image for your composition**

1. Paint your surface with matte medium. Work in small areas, such as a 2" × 2" section.

2. Place your torn or cut papers on the matte medium. Paint over the newly applied papers with more matte medium.

continued on next page

Painting with Papers *continued*

3 Continue this layering of matte medium, collage papers, then matte medium until you have covered the area that you wanted to cover. You can use painted papers to create only a background or an entire planned composition.

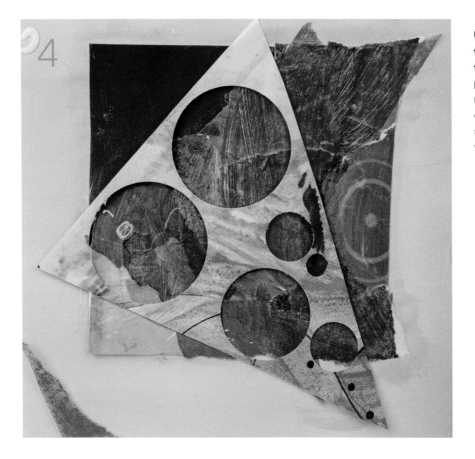

Using this same technique with colored tissue papers or patterned papers can result in a melding of color reminiscent of stained glass or frosted windows.

4 Once the painted papers have dried, experiment with other techniques:

- Bring out the details of your composition, if needed, by adding more layers to define specific areas.

- Paint over the layered papers with a thin layer of gesso so that you still see the background but it becomes a bit more neutral.

- Paint over the layered papers with gesso mixed with an acrylic paint color to unify diverse papers.

- Paint over a section of the papers to bring attention to another section of the collage.

- Create stencils (page 68), and transfer the images onto the collage.

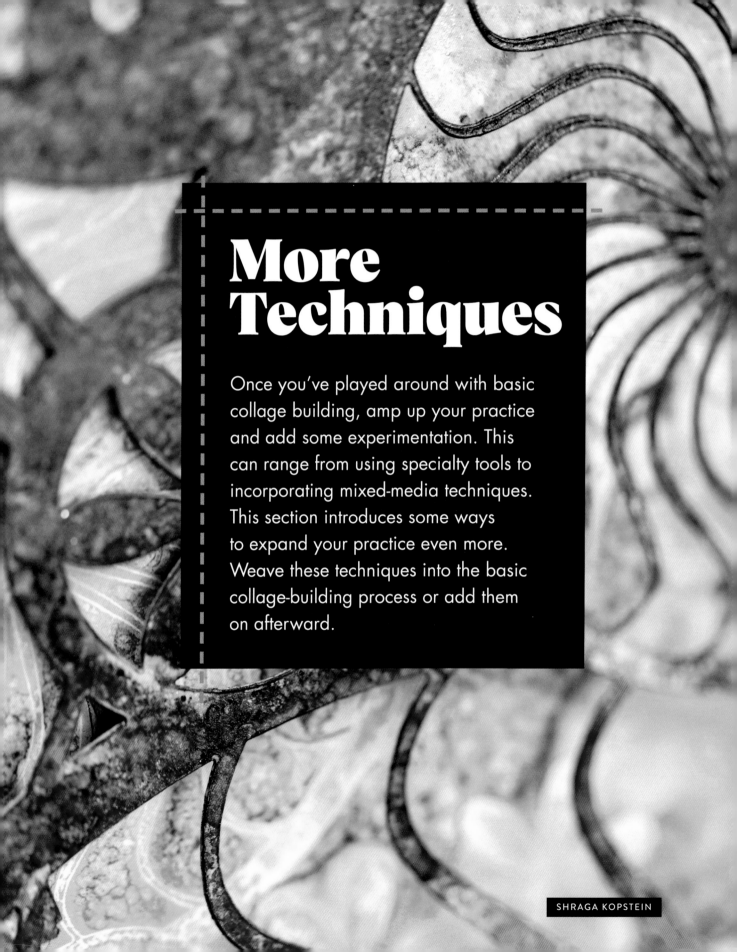

More Techniques

Once you've played around with basic collage building, amp up your practice and add some experimentation. This can range from using specialty tools to incorporating mixed-media techniques. This section introduces some ways to expand your practice even more. Weave these techniques into the basic collage-building process or add them on afterward.

SHRAGA KOPSTEIN

Punches

Punches come in all kinds of sizes and shapes, including circles, squares, butterflies, birds, and more.

TOOLS AND MATERIALS

- **Punches**
- **Paper**
- **Craft knife (optional)**
- **Scissors (optional)**
- **Self-healing cutting mat (optional)**

1 Punch out several forms from different papers. When you punch out a shape, you have the shape (positive space) and the area left behind (negative space). Both are usable in a collage.

2 Try different approaches: Layer together different sizes of punched-out shapes or cut a smaller shape (such as a heart) out of a larger shape (such as a circle).

3 Try using the punch from every angle—right side up, upside down, and sideways—to find the best vantage point. Most punches can be shifted so you see exactly which part of the paper you are punching. Some punches have a cover that you may need to remove to see the paper.

PRO TIP

If a punch doesn't cut all the way through the paper, use your craft knife and cutting mat or your scissors to refine the cut.

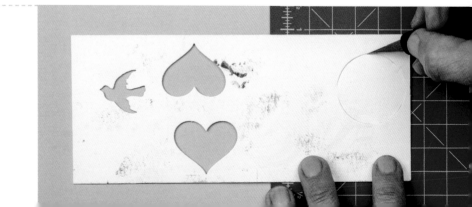

Gesso

Gesso is made from a pigment (usually white or black), calcium carbonate (chalk), and an acrylic medium or binder. It protects the surface and, in the case of canvas, makes it less porous, gives it some flexibility to limit cracking if rolled, and allows paint to adhere better. Here we hack it as a medium for neutralizing a composition, masking a section of the composition, filling in a stencil shape, and other applications. Both black and white gesso are good to have in your toolbox.

TOOLS AND MATERIALS

- **White and/or black gesso**
- **Water (optional)**
- **Brushes**
- **In-progress collage substrate**
- **Stencils (optional)**
- **Cloth rag, paper towel, or sponge**

Neutralizing a Composition

Whether your papers are too shiny, are too saturated, or contain too much color, texture, or brilliance, gesso can help. This is one of the easiest ways to use gesso. Simply paint on some gesso, then wipe it off quickly. I use a cloth rag, but a paper towel or sponge works, too. You can also add some water to the gesso to make it thinner and more transparent. Experiment with how much gesso and/or water you use, how much you wipe, and how much you leave.

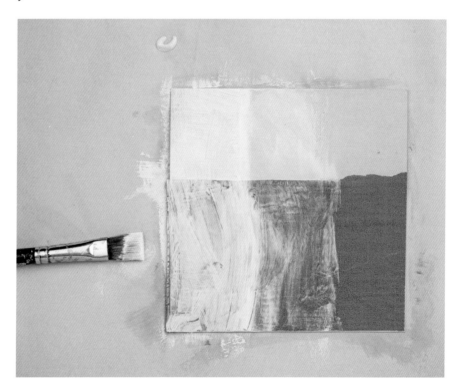

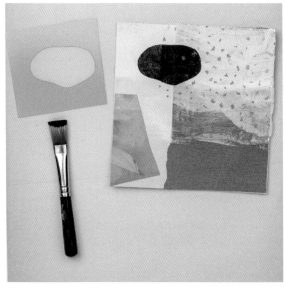

Masking a Section

Use gesso to hide, or mask, a section that you don't like or that you want to conceal for conceptual reasons.

Filling in a Stencil

Trace a precut stencil (yours or a commercially made one) or a shape template onto your collage with a pencil. Remove the stencil, and carefully paint in the outlined shape with gesso.

Add Other Elements

Go freehand and use gesso to add other painterly elements such as dots, lines, or circles to extend a section of the collage's design.

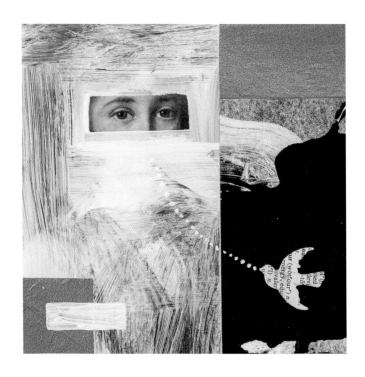

Packing Tape Transfers

You can use clear packing tape to lift toner off toner-based photocopies and some printed materials and then transfer the toner to other items. If you are producing your own image to transfer, it must be a photocopy; this process will not work with inkjet-printed images! Over the years I've found that packing tape from 3M works best.

TOOLS AND MATERIALS

- **Photocopied image or image from a magazine**
- **Clear packing tape**
- **Bone folder**
- **Scissors**
- **Water**
- **Containers for water**
- **Sponge**
- **Clear-drying glue (if needed)**

1 Apply packing tape over the entire image. If your image is large, it's okay to overlap multiple pieces of tape.

2 Burnish with your bone folder or another solid tool. Try using your scissors handles if you don't have a bone folder. Carefully smooth out any air bubbles.

3 Cut around and close to the image if you like. It's easier to cut before you remove the backing paper.

4 Soak the taped image in warm water briefly or dampen the back with a wet sponge.

5 Remove the image from the water and carefully rub the paper side with a damp sponge or your thumb. The paper will start to come off, slowly revealing your translucent image. Continue rubbing until you get all the paper off, dipping your sponge in water as needed to keep the sponge damp. Take care to not rub too hard or you'll lose the delicate lines in some images.

6 Discard paper bits into the trash. You don't want them to clog your drain! Adhere the transferred image to your collage or other surface. If the tape seems to have lost some of its sticking power, add a layer of clear-drying glue to ensure adhesion.

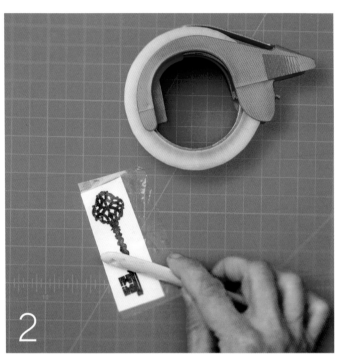

2

4

5

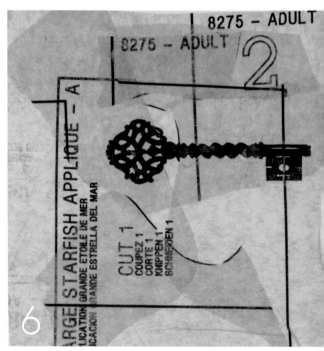

6

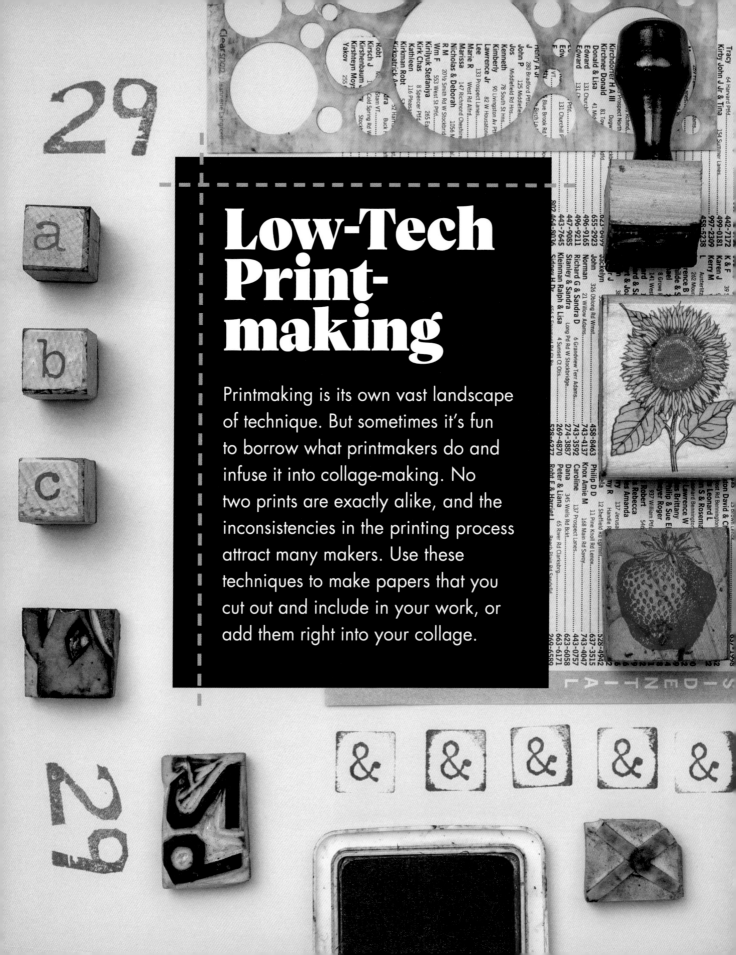

Low-Tech Print-making

Printmaking is its own vast landscape of technique. But sometimes it's fun to borrow what printmakers do and infuse it into collage-making. No two prints are exactly alike, and the inconsistencies in the printing process attract many makers. Use these techniques to make papers that you cut out and include in your work, or add them right into your collage.

Rubber and Other Stamps

Commercially produced rubber stamps number in the thousands, maybe even in the millions. Whatever design you dream up, it's likely been made into a stamp. You can make your own stamps pretty easily from household and readily available materials. The most important thing to remember when making a stamp is that you must cut or carve your image in reverse. While this may not matter for some designs, it will for things like letters and numbers.

Rubber and Other Stamps

MAKE YOUR STAMP

TOOLS AND MATERIALS

- **Soft graphite pencil**
- **Tracing paper**
- **Erasers, corks, or E-Z-Cut printing blocks**
- **Craft knife or linoleum cutter**
- **Pigment-based stamp pad**
- **Test paper**

1 Draw your design onto a piece of tracing paper with your pencil.

2 Flip the design over onto your eraser, cork, or E-Z-Cut material and rub the back of the design until the design transfers. If this method of transferring doesn't work, or if you want to be more fluid, draw directly onto the material you are using for the body of the stamp.

3 Use a craft knife or linoleum cutter to carve your stamp design by cutting away the areas that you *don't* want to print (the white space). Be gentle. You can always carve away more material, but you can't add material back.

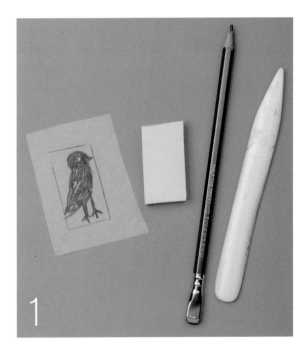

Undercutting

Not Undercutting

PRO TIPS

The most important things to remember when carving are:

- **Carve *away* from yourself. You don't want to get cut!**

- **Do not undercut your image. This weakens the stamp, and detailed sections might break off or not print well. Instead, cut on an outward slope from your design as shown in the lower image above.**

Not Undercutting →

continued on next page

Rubber and Other Stamps *continued*

USE YOUR STAMP

Try out your stamp to see if you need to make any changes or adjustments.

1 Gently press your stamp into the stamp pad. You'll need to practice this to get the right amount of pressure. Too much pressure, and you'll get ink into areas of the stamp you do not want to print; not enough pressure, and your print will be spotty. You may want your print to have that sort of spotty effect, so take care to experiment.

2 Lift the stamp, and place it on your test paper. Press down with your palm to apply even pressure on the stamp.

3 Lift the block and admire your print!

PRO TIP

Anything can become a stamp. For example, some shoes have distinctive and fun patterns. String, cardboard, fabric, and doilies can be stamped, too. Play around with possible stamps to create your own stamped papers that might just find their way into your collages.

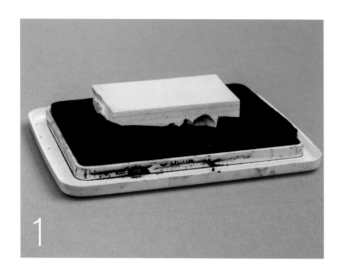

NOTE: You'll need to reink your stamp for every print. When you are finished using the stamp, print with it on a scrap piece of paper until ink no longer remains. These "cleaning" papers can become part of your paper stash to use in a future collage, if you like. After you have stamped off all of the wet ink, clean your stamp as soon as possible with warm water. Blot dry. Some inks will stain your stamps, but as long as you clean the stamp in between uses, those colors will not bleed into your future designs.

Simple Stencils

Simple stencils begin with a drawn or other acquired image that you have manipulated to become your own. These instructions are for a single-color stencil. Begin with basic shapes, then try more complex images as you gain stenciling experience. Once you create your stencils, you can use them to add elements to all kinds of artworks.

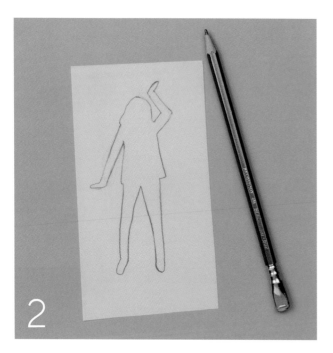

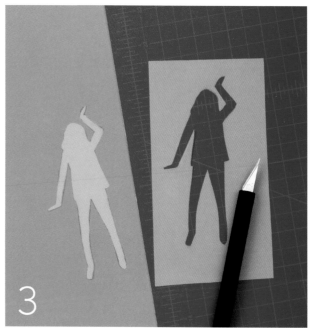

MAKE YOUR STENCIL

TOOLS AND MATERIALS

- **Design or image you like**
- **Pencil or pen**
- **Stencil paper or file folder (most card stock papers will work)**
- **Painter's tape**
- **Craft knife or Versa-Tool (page 9)**
- **Flat piece of glass (if using Versa-Tool)**
- **Watercolor or acrylic paint, gesso, or stamp pad**
- **Stencil brush(es) (optional)**

1 Draw a design or find an image in a magazine or from a photo.

2 Trace your design onto stencil paper, or draw it directly onto a file folder. If you are tracing a design, use painter's tape to secure the design to the stencil paper and prevent slippage.

3 Carefully cut out the stencil using a craft knife or a woodburning tool. If you are using heat, be sure to cut on a piece of glass.

continued on page 71

CUTTING TIPS

- Keep a sharp blade in your cutting knife.

- Cut *away* from corners, not into them.

- Cut the most detailed areas of your stencil first. The more you cut, the flimsier the stencil gets.

- Turn the stencil film—not your hand—to cut.

- On long cuts, hold your knife at a lower angle and farther away from your blade.

- Maintain three points of contact between your hand and the stencil film.

- If you are cutting transparency stencil material, a Versa-Tool or other woodburning tool with knife attachment makes this easy. Just be sure to cut on top of a piece of glass, and never leave the tool unattended while plugged in.

PRO TIP

Whether you want to cut a letter or a complex shape, interior pieces of your stencil will fall out if they aren't connected to an outside layer. For example, think about the letter O. To maintain a center shape, cut connecting points to other parts of the stencil. Keep this in mind when drawing your design.

Simple Stencils *continued*

USE YOUR STENCIL

To stencil an image onto paper, you will need stencil brushes and paint, gesso, or stamp pads. Stamp pads work well because they are high on pigment and low on water (the stenciler's enemy). Watercolors and acrylics also work well; just be sure to tap out the excess liquid before stenciling. Follow the steps below to learn how to create stenciled images with a crisp edge, then practice working with your stencils before using them in a collage.

1 **SECURE THE STENCIL.** Use painter's tape to secure the stencil to the paper or collage. You don't want that stencil to move.

2 **TAP IT OUT.** Every time you add paint or gesso to your brush, tap it out on scrap paper or a rag first to remove excess liquid from the brush. The brush should be almost dry to the touch. If you are using a stamp pad instead of paint, this isn't as big an issue; simply swirl your brush on the stamp pad to load it up with ink.

3 **STENCIL AND SWIRL.** Lightly swirl your brush from the outside to the inside of the stencil. Keep the swirl continuous. Avoid side-to-side movement or applying heavy pressure. It works better to add multiple light layers rather than a single heavy application.

4 **CULTIVATE PATIENCE.** You are going to want to lift up that stencil as soon as you are finished stenciling. Resist this urge. Let the paint, gesso, or ink dry before you lift the stencil.

5 **TAKE CARE.** Clean plastic and heavy Mylar stencils after use with soap and water. If you take care of your stencils, they can last a long time.

PRO TIPS

- **Use doilies, lace, and other found materials as stencils. As long as an item has an opening, it should work as a stencil.**

- **Commercially created stencils are also available. These are great for letters, numbers, and other kinds of forms.**

4

Counties

to change

requires

one

conversio

Adding Text

Text can be used in a collage as the focal point, as a directive for the content, as a mantra, or for so many other purposes. When working with text, consider two things: where to find text and how to use it in the composition.

several cumbersome steps

to

Finding Text

The text can be something you wrote, but it doesn't have to be. Found text can often be more appealing and can lead you to more provocative, thoughtful ways of expression.

1 Look for text in magazines or newspapers, documents from your job, research articles, letters from friends or loved ones, books, encyclopedias and dictionaries, tomes of poetry, old recipes, and shopping lists—really anything with words. Often the more obscure the text, the better. You can also seek out or generate text for collage in your own handwriting, on a typewriter, with a label maker or press-on type, through photocopies or photocopy transfers, with embroidery, or on a letterpress.

2 Once you have found your text, begin to look for words that stand out to you. Let the words and phrases inspire you to form a short poem, full sentences, focus words, or any other kind of combination. There are a few different ways to do this, as described below, or combine the methods.

- **CUT:** Use scissors to cut out words you like, then put the words together to create new meaning.

- **HIGHLIGHT:** Circle words you like. Highlight them with watercolor or colored pencil.

- **BLOCK:** Block out all the words you *don't* want, letting the words you *do* want come to the forefront. Try using solid swaths of color to block out text, or block out words with textured lines, with a single line, or however you decide.

Alphabet Stamps

Alphabet stamps give you the option to create your own words in a predesigned font. As you add type to your collages, keep in mind that typography has personality. If you are creating something edgy, you probably don't want to use a curly typeface.

A Controlled Approach

TOOLS AND MATERIALS

- **Alphabet rubber stamps**
- **Stamp pads**
- **Painter's tape**
- **Waste paper**
- **Collage paper**

1 Choose the letters for your word.

2 Place letter stamps close together in the order of the word.

3 Wrap a piece of painter's tape around the entire word.

4 Press the word into the stamp pad.

5 Print/stamp onto waste paper. If you're happy with your results, commit your word to your collage paper. Otherwise, adjust your word and stamping process as necessary for your desired effect.

A Rogue Approach

1 Choose the letters for your word.

2 Start stamping! Overlap, repeat, under-ink, over-ink. Create words or use the stamps to create textures and patterns.

PRO TIP

Mask an area with gesso. Print on top with waterproof ink, then add watercolor or other mediums to highlight the letters.

Letter Stencils

Letter stencils come in all kinds of shapes and sizes. Regular pens and pencils often don't fit into the curves and lines of letter stencils, especially in the little letters. If you love tiny letters, keep pens and mechanical pencils with skinny tips in your art kit.

TOOLS AND MATERIALS

- **Letter stencils**
- **Collage paper**
- **Ruler**
- **Pens and/or pencils**
- **Washi tape**

NOTE: Painter's tape often can be used instead of washi tape. However, some painter's tape is less reposition-able than washi tape. When you are taping directly onto a final work surface, painter's tape may pull up paper fibers that you don't want to pull up. Though washi tape is more expensive than painter's tape, it also is less likely to disrupt the paper fibers.

1 Determine the text you want to stencil and where on your collage you want to stencil it.

2 Use a ruler to estimate the line on which to stencil. Place a piece of washi tape on that line.

3 Line up the bottom of the letters with the top of your washi tape. With your pen or pencil, begin to stencil your word or words, working carefully and slowly.

4 Remove the washi tape.

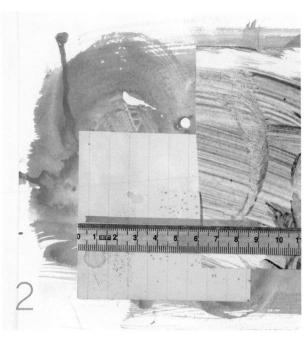

PRO TIP

Some inks will smear when you lift your stencil, so test your materials ahead of time. Practice on some scrap paper before committing to your collage. You never know—the scrap could become part of another collage one day.

Fabric, Feathers, and Found Objects

Most of this book focuses on paper-based collage-making, but every now and then you might want to include something other than paper. Perhaps you collect feathers, butterfly and moth wings, keys, fabric scraps, or another interesting material. Whatever it is, there is always a way to include it in your collage. Here are some ideas to get you started testing and experimenting. You are limited only by your own imagination.

Encapsulate

Encapsulations are like windows that hold little treasures to your collage. Envelope windows, plus the paper that surrounds them, are perfect for this. You can also use clear transparency or packing tape that you cut to size.

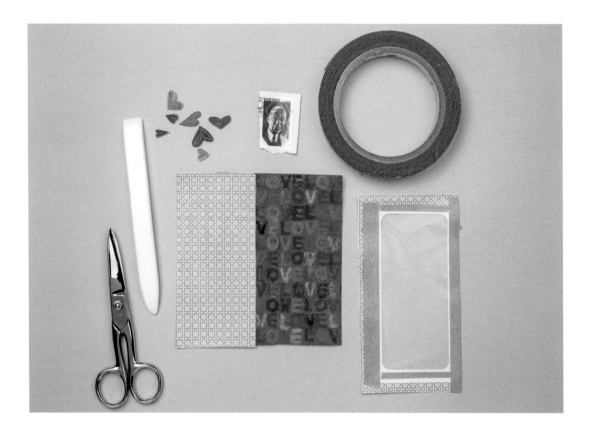

Using Clear Transparency

continued on next page

TOOLS AND MATERIALS

- **Clear transparency or window from an envelope**
- **Fabric, feathers, and found objects**
- **Double-stick tape, glue, or washi tape**

1 Pair your fabric, feather, or found object with a piece of clear transparency or an envelope window that is at least ¼" larger than your object.

Encapsulate *continued*

2　Add double-stick tape or glue to the outside edge of the back of the transparency or envelope window.

3　Lay the item on the collage where you would like to add it, and lay your piece of clear transparency or envelope window over it. Press to secure.

4　Alternatively, you can use washi tape to secure the clear transparency or envelope window on the front side of your collage after you have placed it on top of your object. This is an especially good choice if you have some patterned washi tape.

Using Packing Tape

Cut a piece of packing tape at least as large as the object you would like to add to your collage. Lay the item on the collage where you would like to add it, and lay your piece of tape directly over your object.

Secure

Experiment with other ways to secure fabric, feathers, and found objects onto your collages by stitching, gluing, and making slits and cuts.

TOOLS AND MATERIALS

- **Awl**
- **Needle and thread**
- **Fabric, feathers, and found objects**
- **Various adhesives**

Using Stitching

Use your awl or a needle to poke holes through your collage all the way around the area where you want to secure your item. Thread your needle, tie a knot in the thread, and stitch through the holes to secure the object to the collage. Experiment with stitches that go over and around the item or that make an X or other shapes.

Using Adhesive

Glue your object right onto the collage. PVA glue will work for most porous items that you might want to add to your collage. If your surface is nonporous, you may need to use a hot glue gun or another kind of synthetic adhesive.

ALMA LARROCA

Using Slits and Cuts

Place your object on the collage. Look for corners on your object that can be tucked into the collage. Use your knife to cut short 45-degree slits into your collage paper. Tuck the corners of the object into the collage.

Mixing Mediums

As your collage practice evolves, you may find that you need something else to unify a composition. Perhaps you want to draw attention to an element and deemphasize another. Mixed-media art unites multiple modes in a variety of ways. Collage is part of this, but so are the other techniques described in this book. As you dive in, realize that everything becomes a possibility for your collage or mixed-media work.

Here are some suggestions to get you started:

MADDALENA NOTARDONATO

Painted papers background + magazine + text

CRAIG UPSON

Collage background + gesso stencil

ISABEL ESPANOL

Colored paper background + pen and ink drawing and lettering

MICHELLE DOW

Collage background +
neutralizing layer of gesso +
packing tape transfer

Fabric, Feathers, and Found Objects   **85**

NEW

chapter 3

CENTER OF TURN

FULL

A R

VIEW

mix

made " magical

GLUE

ILLUSTRATED

IN

SEE

COLOR within 3

make

COLIN JOHNSON

All

DATA

Mind Reading

Wonder

Built

55 Prompts to Jump-Start Your Practice

**ANDOMLY OPEN THIS** chapter for a prompt or flip through for inspiration and linger on a spread where the image or text speaks to you. Look at each collage example as fuel for your own creative process, and perhaps advice from a benevolent friend or patron.

Each collage contains an opening suggestion and a prompt that offers ideas on how to make your own version. The examples show how one person expresses their voice and ways of creating; there are endless ways you can move forward in your own collage-making process. Use the examples as inspiration to nurture and develop your own voice. Dive in at random and begin.

Create Parameters

Practice Takes Practice. Some practices stick and are pretty easy to do; others require sustained effort, deliberate action, or clearer definition.

Give yourself parameters, rules, or a prompt. The limitations force your creative juices to make connections that might not be easily made when confronted with unlimited choices.

SOME PARAMETERS INCLUDE:

- Complete the collage in 30 minutes or less.
- Use only scraps from your most recent collage process.
- Take the first three papers from your collage bag and use only those papers.
- Only tear your paper; do not cut.
- Add a stencil element.

There are countless other "rules," or parameters, you can assign to your collage-making. This chapter gives you 55 prompts along with at least one collage made with each prompt in mind, and some words of guidance. Add some of the prompts into your practice, and use them as inspiration for creating your own.

Begin, Again

How to begin? This question might consume your thoughts when faced with a blank sheet of paper and a pile of supplies. You will arrive at this point again and again and again. Your job is to make friends with this feeling of the unknown, and to understand that one of the friends of this unknown is not being attached to the outcome. This is hard. Even if you know this already, it can still be hard. The important thing is to begin. To start. To commence.

Simplicity in design yields solid compositions. This collage uses only five pieces of paper. The bird paired with the lines in the background creates movement. The sliver of yellow on the left balances the large plane of yellow on the right.

PROMPT

1 Create a one-third background by pairing a flat, painted piece of paper with a magazine or brochure cutout that has lots of visual texture.

2 Note the use of the "law of thirds" (see page 39) in your composition.

3 Think about flow and your focal point.

4 Add block-out poetry or a contrasting texture.

Find Your Voice

Whether you are new to the collage-making process or are a veteran, at some point you may begin to ask yourself:

What is my "thing"?

What am I trying to express?

What are my motifs?

What is **MY** way of making?

There's no need to force yourself to find answers. They will start to reveal themselves in time. You will begin to see what you collect, what you gravitate toward. Pay attention. Maybe your "thing" involves patterns and repetition. Patterns can take the form of the same shape repeated in a distinct and orderly way.

PROMPT

Mix patterns and repetition. Overlap and crop to create a new composition. Always remember focal point and eye direction.

Repetition can take one pattern and mix it with other elements to create something altogether new. For example, consider the typewriter keyboard in this collage. Without the letters, the keys form a pattern, with each key overhanging half of the two keys below it. The addition of letters turns the image into something different. You might not even notice the actual pattern of the key shapes.

Translation

When a translator interprets from one language to another, his or her personality finds its way into the work through nuanced decisions of word choice. The way one person reads or sees something will be completely different from how another person reads or sees the same thing. The same is true with art-making. As you start to create, think about what makes you unique. What do you want to call attention to as a creator and maker?

This collage uses a circular composition that begins with the bird shape in the green houselike form. Line, texture, and color move the eye up and around the yellow center, then back to the bird.

PROMPT

1   Create an implied circle through your compositional choices. This might mean adding lines with black and white pens, as pictured here. Perhaps you connect lines found in your paper choices.

2   Choose something to serve as your focal point that will draw your viewer into the composition. (It is okay if you are the only viewer.) Balance the focal point with other color, line, space, and textural choices. Move items around, and let your eye decide when you have found the "correct" place for your focal point.

What Holds You Back

How do you move conversation beyond small talk to the thoughts deep inside your heart and soul, where you are open and able to say things, do things, and make things? How do you get to honest expression? Fear of what others might think can prevent you. Being able to let go of or ignore that fear, or even to go where that fear takes you, leads to the creation of something new and powerful.

What holds us back

In this collage, movement between the subject's eyes, across to the bird, then to the text and back to the eyes creates an implied triangle. The paper overlapping the figure allows the eye to focus more clearly on the bird.

PROMPT

Create an implied movement through your collage using different types of imagery. You don't need much when making a collage. What you do need is a way to connect your imagery together. That might mean blocking out a section using paper and adding some ink lines, as demonstrated here, or perhaps adding another medium. Regardless, find a way to connect your imagery.

Patience

Ever become impatient with the creative process? You want the inspiration, the idea, the "Aha!" moment to arrive. Do you wait passively or actively? Cultivating patience is key to the creative process. Dare to stay where you are, and nurture your creative practice through active waiting. Push yourself to try something new. This can jump-start the creative process, thereby "tricking" the act of waiting that is patience. It doesn't always work, but you can try.

Comb through magazines and old books for images and text to keep ready for your next collage. Make, draw, or do some other kind of creative practice to prime your creative pump. Go for a walk. Ultimately, be patient as you wait. Know that an insight will be revealed from your preparation.

The disembodied eyes in this collage are examples of jump-starting the creative process by trying something different.

PROMPT

1   Build a colorful background.

2   Layer a window or other opening cutout on top.

3   Add an element to your work that is unusual for you.

55 Prompts to Jump-Start Your Practice   **95**

Go Big

It can be super gratifying to get caught up in tiny details. For example, when drawing a portrait, it's easy to all of a sudden have completed one of the eyes before really figuring out the full composition. The same can be true for project management, cooking, home design, really everything. When this happens to you, circle back to the big picture before you narrow it down into the tiny tasks needed to complete the project. Your imagination and dreams thrive in big, open spaces. Envision that big idea! Then break it down into manageable parts.

Kaci Smith's creative process begins **BIG** and then gets broken into smaller works of art. Read on.

ARTIST STATEMENT
Kaci Smith

"Collage has been an entry point back into my art practice after many years away from it, and I like to draw on my textile design background when working with pattern and color. My collage work consists of a mixture of painted paper (that I create), fabric, discarded scraps and ephemera, book pages, commercial wallcoverings, and whatever else I find. No catalog or piece of mail I receive gets past my 'Can I collage that?' eye. I then augment the layouts with paint and mark-making. I also love to use vintage fabric printing blocks in the layers.

To create the painted papers that I then use in my collages, I start by covering a wall with large sheets of paper to establish a surface. I then completely fill that paper with acrylic and spray paint, trying different mark-making and masking techniques and all kinds of color combinations. I don't worry about the end result because I eventually tear the large sheets of paper randomly into smaller pieces. Each of those scraps then feels like something wonderful that I've discovered.

This way of working gives me a unique result and provides me with lots of bits and pieces to work with when I transition back to assembling my collage. I find that working big is a helpful way to bring a flow and spontaneity into my small finished pieces."

PROMPT

1   Cover a wall with paper.

2   Gather up several paint colors and brushes, and start layering on colors and patterns.

3   Let drips happen, and have fun.

How to Change Your Mind

It's easy to stay in your comfort zone, especially as you get older. Change it up. Eat something different for breakfast. Drive a different way to work or to the place where you volunteer. Make a date with that person you just met. Do something to break patterns, especially ones that do not benefit you or ones that, if broken, may lead you to your best possible self.

In this collage the bird is positioned with most of it cropped out of the composition to suggest that ideas often exist beyond what we can see.

PROMPT

Start with an image that you use regularly and do something different to it. Crop it, zoom in, pair it with something opposite or unusual. Use it in a way different from your usual practice.

HEATHER POLK

PAMELA TOWNS

One Size Does Not Fit All

If you've ever tried on one of those "one size fits all" shirts or dresses, you know what a farce that is. The same holds true for an art practice. Your creative practice will look completely different from someone else's practice. If you don't already know your own context, your personal visual language, and your preferred ways of using the mediums, start exploring. Maybe you like humor and irony. Perhaps you like to weave in religious or devotional imagery. You may prefer to shock and question. Whatever it is, keep chasing it.

PROMPT

Create a collage that incorporates the patterns and textures from security envelopes. It can be part of the background or foreground or used as an accent.

There is a trove of wonderfulness in your mail, especially in those security envelopes. Patterns and visual textures abound! Start collecting those envelopes. Keep the windows too; those transparent papers can add a different kind of dimension and element to your work.

Who or What Guides You?

Whether you find faith in a spiritual practice, your community, nature, or your work, you likely have something—or someone—that guides you. Maybe it's a teacher, a friend, or an important leader. Or possibly it's a prayer that you repeat over and over. Whatever or whoever they are, guides are important in our lives. Often guides can appear in the most unlikely places and shine a new light on your situation. Maybe it's an encounter with a stranger who empathizes with your child's meltdown at the supermarket. It could be a long-trusted friend who knows exactly what to say to you. Channel these guides, and create your own.

Undoubtedly you have a treasure trove of support and guidance that lives inside you, waiting to be revealed through your artistic practice. To coax that out, follow the lead of artist and writer *Suzi Banks Baum*, who creates figures in her journal using an intuitive collage process.

ARTIST STATEMENT

Suzi Banks Baum

"I collage figures of women who appear as soothsayers, guides, elders, or oracle bearers. I use a collage process of laying together images of two different women's figures, each torn in half. I try to match either the hairlines or shoulder lines. The selection process is intuitive. I see two different images and sense that by combining one half of each image, they could conjure a figure that bears some of their original contours but becomes something altogether new."

PROMPT

1 Write secrets, desires, private thoughts, or dreams on the substrate with a pencil. You will glue on top of this writing, burying it into the essence of the collage. When you embed words into the making of the collage in this way, the collage becomes its own kind of prayer. Experiment with writing what your guides might say to you in an hour of need.

2 Glue down the halves of two figures. Use black gesso to reduce imagery around the combined figure.

3 Layer black gesso, acrylic, and gouache to blend the two halves into one figure.

4 Use graphite pencils to give shape, and colored pencils, paint, and gel pens to finish the face.

5 Once the collaged figure becomes a whole and singular image, let some time pass, then go back and add new text about who or what guides you. This will serve as a top decorative layer of your collage.

PRO TIP A collage can carry layers of meaning that help you digest experience and integrate learning.

ASK

The mantra "If you don't ask, you don't get" circles in my mind when I want or need something from someone. It could simply be directions to the restroom. Or it could be help with a project, a raise, a promotion, a divorce. Embarrassment, shame, and fear often cloud the way to the ask. When you hold back from asking, you deny that part of you that knows what it wants. Remember, the worst thing that can happen is that someone will say no, or maybe yes.

The harvested text in this collage reads, "Ask. Frivolous demands survive."

PROMPT

1   Build a background. Divide your composition into thirds. Consider how pattern and repetition impact your overall design.

2   Think about the number 3. Use the same image three times.

3   Harvest some words from your text collections. Create a three-word sentence that expresses your own ask and incorporate it into your collage.

ANTHONY ZINONOS

Disrupt

Do you ever struggle between wanting to maintain the status quo and wanting to disrupt everything around you? Is complacency, comfort, or being at ease bad? Do movement and change have to be driving forces? Is there peace in stability? Or is mobility better? The body typically longs for both stability and mobility exercises. One without the other can lead to injury, discomfort, and even pain. Disruption for one person might be the status quo for another person. The next time you ask yourself what's more important—disrupting the status quo or finding peace in the comfort of routine—try both!

PROMPT

Break out of a pattern. Let repetition of a shape begin in an ordered manner and then dissolve into something else. Bonus if you use gold from a candy wrapper or other packaging.

Find Your Antlers

"Find your antlers" is a mantra I use to help move myself out of negativity. I coined the phrase when I found a full rack of antlers, discarded from a caribou, during a National Park Service artist residency in Denali National Park & Preserve. Discovering that full rack of antlers instantly catapulted me out of my funk.

Think of your own version of this, a moment when a person, place, or thing pushed you out of your negativity. How can you weave that into your collage practice? While antlers do not appear in my work often, when they do, I am reminding myself to shift my perspective.

Every artist develops his or her own visual language over time. Colors. Textures. Patterns. Motifs. One of the goals of this book is for you to pay attention to your visual likes and dislikes. You may find you like watch faces, buildings, or sunsets. Gather and collect those images. Build image files to hold your collections for when you need a certain image in a collage. Occasionally other kinds of images will find their way into your work. Let them. Acknowledge them, for they might provide the visual or conceptual variety that your collage needs.

PROMPT

1 Create a background. Perhaps it's a piece of block-out poetry; maybe it's a landscape.

2 Layer your own version of "antlers" into the collage. Do they float? Maybe they frame? Try a few things out before committing to a composition.

Use Your Hands

I love my hands. I could not do my work without them. I try very hard to take care of them, protect them, respect them, and express my gratitude for them. They have certainly gotten in the way of sharp and heavy equipment but thankfully haven't suffered too much damage. You might feel similarly grateful for your hands, or your eyes, or maybe your ears. Our senses direct how we experience our world and surroundings, and they allow us to dig into the work of the artist.

When I look at the prominent lines in my hands, I equate them with life lessons that I need to learn. Certain lessons seem to circle back to me repeatedly. I assimilate some, but others repeat over and over, while new ones mix in.

The text toward the top of this collage says, "Let It Breathe," which parallels a phrase many people say to themselves: "Let it go."

PROMPT

1 Trace your hand onto patterned paper. This is a great prompt to do 10 or more times. Think of all the different papers you could use: magazine pages, painted papers, newsprint, and more.

2 Layer it between background papers and foreground papers. You decide what that means.

3 Add some text.

BILLY RENKL

Play with Memory

When I was small I had a pair of vibrant, electric, tangerine pants that I wanted to put on every day. Those orange pants transformed my little girl legs into magic. My mom would "bribe" me to put on a dress or something else when we went out by saying I could put my orange awesomeness back on as soon as we got home. The girl in this collage reminds me of myself as a little girl. What images remind you of your childhood?

This collage combines paste papers, magazine pages, and children's book text and images. The words and phrases in your collage could also be handwritten or stenciled.

PROMPT

1 Dive into your memories. Look for a picture, pattern, or text that reminds you of your childhood. Perhaps you choose an actual photograph. Use that as a starting point.

2 Experiment with creating layers with flat painted papers and dimensional magazine papers. Overlap them to create a sense of depth.

3 Add some text.

I Know, I'm Ready, I Can

Phrases of empowerment can elevate a collage to become a daily reminder or a mantra that you want to see over and over again. These phrases invite you to frame and reframe your thoughts toward the vision you have for yourself. Collect fortune cookie messages or tea bag labels, or write down words of wisdom as you come across them. Keep your favorites in a little envelope in your collage stash.

Blue fencelike pickets serve as the highlight element in the foreground.

PROMPT

1 Build a neutral background.

2 Layer different kinds of frames in the midground.

3 Add some kind of highlight element for your foreground.

4 Incorporate a tea bag quote, a fortune cookie message, or other snippet of text in your collage.

RUBY SILVIOUS

There's Never a Perfect Time

I often hear friends and students say they never have time to make artwork. I get it. We are all busy. Children need parents. Parents need caretakers. Work, volunteer obligations, and other responsibilities fill nearly every hour of the day. Creative practice feels impossible, maybe even selfish.

Embrace the fact that there may never be a perfect time to schedule creative practice. That acknowledgment might be exactly what you need to find 5 or 10 minutes that you can cobble together into a creative practice. These short, stolen moments are enough to ignite our ability to find longer periods of time. And if you miss a day, or fail to schedule your creative practice, you can always begin again. There's no shame in that.

Some of the best artwork comes from the reworking, cutting up, or so-called destroying of old or past artworks. You can frame this as a fresh start!

PROMPT

Cut out sections of an old drawing or old print and reassemble in a new arrangement.

OR

Slice an artwork into strips and weave those parts together. Layer that into a new collage, or let it speak for itself.

Self-Portrait as Mirror

How often do you look in the mirror and focus on the negative instead of appreciating the gorgeous person in front of you? Maybe you think, "I'm too fat." "I'm too thin." "Look at those lines; I have so many wrinkles." "I hate my nose." "My ears stick out." We wouldn't say those things to our beloved family members, friends, or students, right? So why do we say them to ourselves?

To turn off the negative self-talk and focus on the good, ask yourself what you like about what you see in the mirror. Maybe it's your facial features or your hands. Maybe you have strong legs or a set of biceps aching to push up. Appreciate your softness. Appreciate your edges. Think about what you really want that mirror to reflect back to you.

Evita Tezeno makes gorgeous portraits of herself and others using painted papers she has created, often including another element—such as flowers or a dreamy background—to further tell the story. What story can you tell with your portrait?

ARTIST STATEMENT
Evita Tezeno

"I hold close the memories of days gone by. I relish the time before there was Wi-Fi, cell phones, and so many other visual distractions. Longing for the simple things of yesterday, I hear the silent echoes that seemingly dance in my visual consciousness. Those images are the embodiment of my art practice, a viewable narrative, a rearview mirror perspective of my life experiences.

My stories are told in the materials that I choose, the textures that I combine, and the colors that create the compositions in my work. I use vibrant color, layered surfaces, and lush textures to make intriguing and inviting portraits. The process is a journey, and the end point is always well planned. It usually begins with painting paper using watercolor, acrylic, crayon, and various other mediums and techniques. Starting with a preplanned sketch, I use tracing paper to trace shapes. I then cut out the patterns from my painted papers and arrange them like a puzzle to form the facial structure, clothing, and various parts of the figure."

PROMPT

You are going to make a portrait! Hopefully of yourself, but it can be of anyone. Perhaps you make an oversized head on a tiny body, or you exaggerate the size of certain features. Play. Have fun.

1 Gather colored papers. These can be papers you cut out of magazines or papers you've painted yourself.

2 Draw a preliminary sketch of your portrait subject. If you're making a portrait of yourself, you can either look in a mirror and sketch onto a piece of paper or print out a picture of yourself and then trace over it to get your sketch.

3 Place tracing paper on top of your sketch, and draw various shapes and patterns. Layer the tracing over your gathered papers, then cut out patterns from the colored or painted papers.

4 Put your shapes together to form your figure.

Let Your Light Shine

Ever struggle with managing anxiety? Just as pain does, anxiety manifests itself in the brain. Doctors have developed strategies to change the way the brain fires when in pain, and I let this technique inspire my own way of dealing with anxiety. I imagine the area in my brain where anxiety lives, typically around my third eye (the area between my eyebrows). I focus on that point and visualize a deep blue light, which represents my anxiety and gets smaller and smaller until it disappears. By extinguishing the hold of my anxiety, I am able to let the light of myself shine forward.

You can add your stencil shape to any background. This collage highlights those lovely patterns on the inside of envelopes.

PROMPT

1 Design and cut a new stencil. Be careful as you cut out the stencil material so that you can actually get two usable stencils—one for making a so-called negative shape (the area "around" a shape), and one for making a positive shape (the shape itself).

2 Play with both stencils to see how the negative and positive shapes differ.

3 Add either shape or both stenciled shapes onto a background.

CONNY LEHMANN

It Is Solved by Walking

I aim to balance out the time I spend using technology by spending an equal amount of time making art or being in nature. It's not an easy feat these days, and one that I do not accomplish regularly. Sometimes I feel I am getting close, and then a project is due or I must create a new lesson plan, or I get sucked into my email and social media.

I use a timer to help me spend as little time as possible doing these computer tasks. That helps. But I often come back to one of my favorite phrases, "Solvitur ambulando," or, "It is solved by walking," which is attributed to Saint Augustine. Often when I am stuck on a problem or can't seem to make progress with an idea, I find it helps to go for a walk and let my mind wander among the branches and leaves.

This collage mixes a few different types of mediums.

PROMPT

1 Build out a patterned background, whatever you like.

2 Use pen to stencil in text and pathways to represent your walking. These inked pathways often look like stitching. You can also intentionally mimic stitching in collages by drawing dashed lines with your pen or pencil.

What Yes Comes from No?

Leaning into your creative practice means saying no to other things, but that can look different for each person. Perhaps leaning in for you reminds you to step forward and engage with difficult experiences and situations. Maybe it encourages you to start. Possibly you use leaning in as a way to challenge yourself to create artworks about social injustices or to create a new piece of art before you cut up a beloved artwork. Whatever leaning in means to you, go where the fear takes you.

In this collage, the central focal point is the circle on the chest of the human figure.

PROMPT

1 Build a background that feels like a landscape; include a sun or moon as an additional feature, if you'd like.

2 Add a focal point.

3 Add a final layer made from strips of a previously discarded artwork. Turn each no into a yes.

Get Comfortable with Being Uncomfortable

Creating and making often can feel uncomfortable. Something doesn't work, it's not what you envisioned in your head, you have absolutely no ideas, or you feel lackluster and uninspired. Perhaps you want to express an idea that makes you feel vulnerable or puts you outside your comfort zone.

Think about the times outside your art practice when you've been uncomfortable. Most likely, the more you made peace with those feelings of discomfort, the less intense they were. You even may have found a place of acceptance that allowed you to move forward and make progress. The same is true within your art practice. Alternatively, intentionally making yourself uncomfortable in your creating and making, and learning how to breathe into that feeling, can make it easier to tolerate the uncomfortable feelings in other moments in your life.

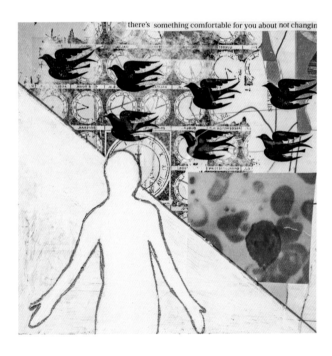

PROMPT

1 Take an unsuccessful beginning of a collage—preferably one that you dislike so much it makes you uncomfortable. If you don't have one, begin with papers that you don't really like.

2 Mask an area of the collage using a plain piece of paper of any color.

3 Add other elements, such as transfers, realistic images, flat patterns, or anything else to link the masked and nonmasked areas together. Consider how these additional elements emphasize your focal point.

Envision

Athletes and artists share many common practices, including visioning. Athletes practice in their minds just as much as in their bodies. They imagine themselves completing their particular athletic feat, whether it's a running race, a gymnastic routine, or playing in a team sport. The same is true for artists. What do you imagine yourself making? Can you weave some of those ideas into your collage? One way to do this is by incorporating text, sometimes just as snippets, other times creating a background from a whole dictionary page.

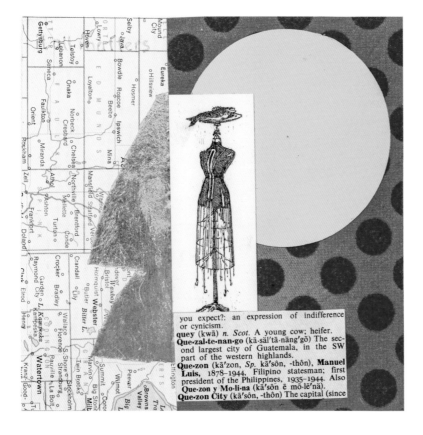

PROMPT

1   Use watercolor, colored pencil, pen, and/or transparent papers to highlight words you consider "important" on one or more dictionary pages.

2   Decide whether the entire dictionary page will serve as your background or you want to use only a snippet of the page. Build your background accordingly.

3   Add one or more other elements. Think about how the additional element(s) continue(s) to tell your story.

Embrace Fluidity

Do you have friends or colleagues who seem to manage whatever comes at them with the utmost grace? You know, the ones who travel, parent, caretake their own parents, win awards, and still do their day job with what looks like ease? What is their secret?

With lots of practice, it can become second nature. You'll need to accept the situation, turn yourself over to it, and, most importantly, not resist it. Resistance erupts into frustration. To embrace fluidity means embracing the late nights and early mornings, the suitcases, and the uncertainty. When you relax into the challenge of the moment, so many things improve.

PROMPT

1 Page through some magazines. Find a shape you like, and make that shape into a stencil.

2 Create a background that will become a frame for your foreground focal point.

3 Add another layer—perhaps incorporating a square or a circle—to serve as a frame for your focal point.

4 On top of your background, use gesso to fill in the shape of your magazine stencil to create a focal point.

5 Add a bird to the composition, just for fun!

PRO TIP

Stencils come in all kinds of shapes and sizes: typography, simple shapes, complicated shapes. You can buy them; you can make them (see page 68). One of my favorite ways of making a stencil is by finding a shape or figure that I like in a magazine and using that as a stencil. These figurative stencils are found throughout my collage work. Sometimes I use them with gesso, as I do here, to mask out the background and allow the figure to become part of the foreground. Sometimes I cut another figure from the original magazine shape. Keep your eye out for possibilities.

LAURA WEILER

What Passes through Your Hands?

ARTIST STATEMENT
Heather Matthew

If you are like me, a ton of paper likely passes through your hands every day. Some you probably don't even pay attention to—it just goes right into the trash or the recycling. But every single item could be fodder for creativity. Keep an envelope or plastic bag with you so you have somewhere to store papers you encounter. Ignore nothing. You never know how the material might translate into a collage. It might get buried with another medium, but who cares? You'll know it's there and it will ground the memory of a particular day into your collage. Heather Matthew excels at this, using her daily finds at home and when abroad to create. Try it yourself.

"In 2010, I began an ongoing project to document my life through daily collages. These small collages use recycled papers and everyday materials such as train tickets, found text, postage stamps, and my own discarded prints and paintings. Some years I included stitching in the collages as an added challenge. Other years I created concertina books for each month, with one page for each day of the month. When I was traveling with only a backpack for three months, I used shipping tags as my substrates.

Creating daily artworks not only helps me document my life but also serves as a solid creative habit that I use to springboard my ideas into other works. When my studio was flooded in 2017, I collaged together mud-stained and flood-marked papers to tell a story of resilience and climate crisis. And I documented my travels through Europe in 2018 by creating 91 collaged postcards.

While some of my collages express my political beliefs, I also use collage to explore human connection. These actions express and propose a message of hope, that our small daily offerings can help heal the world."

PROMPT

1 Collect papers from your day, your week, or a particular trip. Your papers can include bags, receipts, tickets, ephemera, drawings from your children, or whatever else you want.

2 Determine your substrate. Will you use something from the found papers or something else?

3 From your collection of found papers create one or more collages that document the particular day, month, or experience.

Find Forgiveness

Think about a time you have felt "wronged" by someone and your righteous outrage became your only morsel of focus. That outrage can become quite a burden, but the only person who suffers is you, the person who carries the outrage. To find forgiveness you must let go of your hurt. Easier said than done. Time becomes your friend in moments like these. You might also imagine placing your anger in the beak of a bird, as she flies far away, as in this collage.

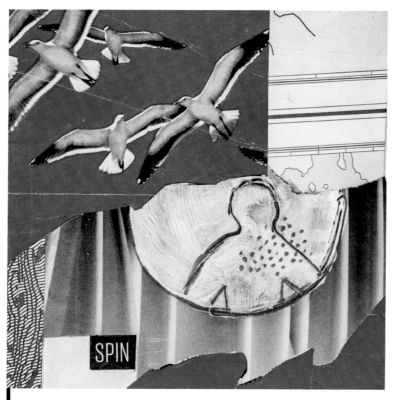

PROMPT

For your collage, combine three items:

- Something realistic that represents an emotion you would like to let go of or forgive
- Something flat to serve as your background or backdrop
- Gesso, graphite, or other mixed mediums to create a mark, pattern, or other form that suggests letting something go

In this collage, seagulls on a blue background represent a realistic item; the map and the paper from the inside of an envelope are flat items; and the gesso and graphite figure in the circle are mixed mediums. Notice how the seagull image is cut (part of the blue background is at the bottom right corner of the collage) and both parts are used to frame the interior mixed-media image.

IVALDO FERREIRA

Revise or Censor?

Have you ever made a collage that felt too personal and revealing? You can collage over the area you think is especially intimate or mask it with some gesso. Is this a revision? Or is it censorship? Either way, the collage will hold a secret that the naked eye would never guess.

live with all your heart

PROMPT

1   Write your story, wish, or dream on your substrate as an offering to your own creative practice.

2   Begin to layer over your text with colored papers of various shapes and sheens.

3   Use a little gesso to neutralize the papers and then add more papers or another medium to create your focal point.

Useless Anxiety

I once knew a no-nonsense priest who offered a prayer that has become one of my mantras: "Protect us from useless anxiety." I return to these words again and again.

What patterns of thought cloud your mind? What thoughts loop endlessly like a scratched record? What can you learn from the repetition? Is the anxiety something you can change? If so, don't wait, do it now. Then watch the anxiety slip away.

If the anxiety is something you can't change or is completely out of your control, name it. Then craft a collage to identify it. Do your best to make it your friend. Face it, and then it might just disappear.

PROMPT

Use lines to connect and divide a collage. The lines can be curved or straight, implied or implicit. Overwhelm the page with lines, similar to how anxiety can overwhelm your mind.

Wander

I remember being scolded when I was a little girl for getting lost. I was never lost, though, just wandering. Over time, I developed confidence in my ability to wander without getting lost. I let myself follow a color or the way the light shifted or someone who looked appealing, and I always trusted that I would return to my starting point. This confidence emboldened me to explore an ever-widening circle of the world and to approach my work as an artist with the same expansive style.

How can you wander as an artist? What would that look like? Try experimentation and trust. Follow the tangent that your creative mind wants to take, but most importantly, detach from the outcome. Wandering is never about a destination, but about what happens within the moment of the wander.

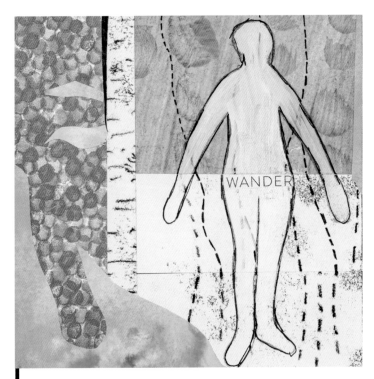

The red and green complementary colors on the left side of the collage help balance the rest of the composition.

PROMPT

1 Wander through your papers for complementary colors. When paired together they can create a sharp contrast or help balance another part of a composition.

2 Choose small and large pieces. Overlap and stack them. Follow the tangent that the papers want to take.

3 Add a focal point and other textures to unify your composition.

BRANDON BREWER

I Don't Have to Do This, I Get to Do This

Anyone in my family who reads this would be shocked to learn that I am cheerful getting out of bed in the morning. When I was young, my dad would pretend to be a crane and pull me out of bed to overcome my desire to luxuriate between the sheets. As an adult, I've learned that the morning holds precious moments. I wake, then complete my various rituals: writing and reflection, review of the day's events, exercise, home caring tasks. As I get older, these routines not only normalize my days but also open up space and possibility in my brain, allowing the light of creativity to enter.

When collaging, consider not only the content of the words you find, but also their appearance. Some Os are perfectly round; others are more oval. Stacked together, letters and words can become new shapes, imaginative creatures, or whatever else you want them to be.

PROMPT

1. Choose a background that you don't really like. Add gesso, other papers, or really anything; you want to turn it into something that pleases you.

2. Use text to create an image. Cut out big letters. What shapes do they suggest?

3. Combine the letters to craft something new.

Deliberate Practice

I make a letterpress card that says, "Practice Takes Practice." Anyone who commits to daily exercise, yoga, making, or anything involving skill knows this to be true. A practice takes commitment, regular preparation and rehearsal, and focused attention on continual skill refinement. In some disciplines, you must accumulate 10,000 hours of "deliberate practice" to be considered accomplished.

Deliberate practice involves noticing areas that need improvement, repeating the drills, and working on the hard stuff. It is then, and only then, that one advances to the next challenge. You can apply this same approach to anything in life. When you embrace the beginner's mindset, accept the willingness to be uncomfortable, and commit to focusing on the areas that need attention, you will persevere. You will see change.

To establish this kind of deliberate practice in your studio, commit to making something every day. Force yourself to make quickly sometimes. Have multiple compositions going at once. Pay attention to focal point, how the eye moves through the composition, balance, and the relationship between flat and dimensional images. Make and evaluate, but keep the judge at bay. Critique only the very formal elements of the composition.

PROMPT

Challenge yourself to work on three to five collages *at the same time*. Begin by setting up your substrate for each collage, then gather your materials and begin. As you move through each step and each collage, note what comes up for you in the practice. Do you need to be more mindful about gluing? More attentive to emphasizing the focal point? More deliberate in your overall composition development? These are the kinds of questions to ask yourself when you are working with deliberate practice.

1   Tear paper and layer one piece on top of another layer. Repeat a few times.

2   Visually stitch the pieces back together using small black lines.

3   Add another element or two to create both a focal point and a reason for your viewer's eye to move around the composition.

Join a Challenge

Artists often create in the privacy of their homes and studios. Some live in remote areas, where artistic communities might be hard to come by. Others desire connection but don't have the time, energy, or resources to meet in person.

Hello, internet. Online challenges that create community, provide inspiration, and encourage people to work together abound. These external challenges can make a difference in your creative life because they prompt you to explore a theme or technique you wouldn't necessarily choose for yourself. By forcing you outside your comfort zone, they sometimes lead to unexpected creative connections. They might even launch you into self-discovery or ways of making that are not only new to you, but that you absolutely adore.

Adam Hutcheson and Aaron Gordon (known on social media as @it_still_moves and @ctrlx.ctrlv, respectively) have created a weekly collage challenge through their GlueTogether account on Instagram. It's a great community of makers, and anyone can join in.

ARTIST STATEMENT
GlueTogether

"We started GlueTogether on Instagram when we realized that we were sourcing imagery from many of the same magazines, so we decided to challenge each other to make collages using the same issue of *National Geographic*. The first theme of the GlueTogether challenge was the July 1960 *National Geographic*. That inaugural week we recruited only one other artist, Eric Toscano, but realized this could be a great way to galvanize collage artists around the globe.

Sure enough, submissions started pouring in. Weekly themes have included Nostalgia, Eyes, and War. There have also been technique-based themes—such as Abstract or Ripped & Torn—that challenge artists to step out of their comfort zones. The results have been incredible pieces of art, yielding creative growth from all participating artists.

GlueTogether is an open invitation for anyone on Instagram to challenge themselves through the medium of collage. Anyone interested, regardless of experience level, can submit artwork using the hashtag #GlueTogether. As the curators of the page, we feature collage art that speaks to us, while also touching on the weekly theme. Browse our Instagram account, @gluetogether, and you will find vastly different interpretations of the same weekly theme. But the best part, regardless of the many geographic or cultural differences, is that everyone is speaking the same language, spoken in paper, scissors, and glue."

PROMPT

Go to @gluetogether on Instagram. Examine the collages posted. Explore the weekly themes. Then use some of the techniques learned in this book to create a collage. Share your finished composition with the hashtags #GlueTogether and #CollageYourLife.

ADAM HUTCHESON

Strength Is Subtle

Harvesting text through cut, highlight, and block-out poetry is a great technique for manipulating words. Sometimes it's much easier to start with someone else's words than it is to try piecing together your own. Old books from thrift shops or vintage stores can provide the medium for rich word experiments. Browse for obscure and forgotten texts, often the older the better.

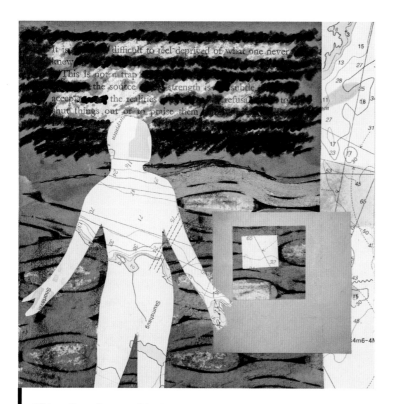

PROMPT

1   Decide on a limited color palette.

2   Begin with a text that appeals to you, and in it look for words that stand out to you. Let the words and phrases inspire you to form a short poem, full sentences, focus words, or any other kind of combination of text. Manipulate the text using cut, highlight, or block-out poetry. Add it to the collage.

3   Add a frame to an unnoticed section of your composition.

This collage features block-out poetry. Here's the new text:

**It is   difficult to feel deprived of what one never
knew
This is not a trap
the source   of strength is subtle
accept the realities   refuse to
shut things out or to praise them**

Face It

Negativity roots in fear. Fear of the unknown, fear of authority, fear of talking to somebody you don't know, fear of someone who thinks differently from you, fear of making art. Facing the fear requires courage and love. Facing fear in your art practice can fuel the way toward facing fear in other parts of your life. Practice this today. Try something that scares you.

When I'm on the Mekong ferry, the day of the black
[...] veranda [...]
[...] Everything has grown up all around us. [...]
[...] is [...]
[...] love [...]

LAURA DIDYK

PROMPT

1   Play with block-out poetry. You can choose a random paragraph of text or be more intentional about it. Use a black pen or black ink, and mark out all the areas you want to eliminate. You can use watercolor or colored pencil to highlight the words you want to keep.

2   Combine your block-out poetry with other papers. Choose a color to help link elements together.

Block-out poetry asks you to "destroy" someone else's words to create something new. It takes courage to highlight what to keep and mark what to block. To begin, try circling words that empower you or words that form a new sentence or statement that has an entirely different meaning.

Sometimes the workshops cross the line between collage and street art, with participants creating collage on public lampposts to brighten up the neighborhood.

Collage with Others

It's really fun to make collages with a group of people. The act of cutting and pasting ignites conversation and collaboration and helps to break down barriers. Working around others gives you the chance to explore new ideas, learn new techniques, and share your own tips and tricks. Pay it forward and pay it back all at once!

Kike Congrains takes the practice of collaging with others to another level. He created the Instagram account @CollageWave to popularize collage in Peru. It has grown into a global platform that unites collage artists from around the world and led him to teach collage workshops in underserved communities in Lima, Peru.

ARTIST STATEMENT
Kike Congrains

"I teach collage workshops to under-resourced children in the outskirts of Lima, Peru, working with organizations that seek to improve the quality of life in their communities. To ensure the collage workshops are available to everyone, I provide the materials, including magazines, scissors, and glue. Instead of giving kids instructions, I let workshop participants find their flow. I get right in there with them and get my hands dirty, too. The finished pieces offer a glimpse inside each child's mind through the story they've created."

PROMPT

Reach out to arts organizations in your community, and find one with an in-person or online collage club. Join one and create with others! Maybe it will lead you to teaching your own workshops someday.

Open for Fun

When was the last time you had fun? What does fun even mean for you? What might fun look like when you're thinking about it as an artist? Do you like to get messy or stay clean and organized? Do you like precision or grit? Maybe you ping-pong back and forth between the two.

Maybe you think of the very act of making art as your fun. How could you make it even more fun? No matter what fun looks like to you, the important thing is opening yourself up to fun and possibility. Try putting "play" into your calendar. What's stopping you from planning a little fun?

PROMPT

Gesso can help integrate an image into a composition. Play with this magical medium in its white or black form.

1   Find an image that has lines or shapes that extend off the composition. Build that as one of the top layers of your composition.

2   Use gesso to extend and overlap that design into the remainder of the composition.

Walk the Line

There are moments in life when you walk the line between good and evil, positive and negative, joy and sorrow, or a myriad of other dualities. Staying in that middle space becomes its own challenge. So much of life exists on continuums of extremes that dictate choices. You may even be forced to choose something that makes you uncomfortable. What lines do you walk?

PROMPT

1 Build layers on top of a found map so that the original map details are somewhat obscured. Mix collage, stencil, stamps, ink, or whatever you like to walk the line between obliterating the map and enhancing it.

2 Find a shape in a magazine that you like. It can be a figure but doesn't have to be; it should just be something that you really like.

3 Use stencil material, if you have it, or an old file folder to create a stencil from your shape. Stencil the shape just to the left or right of center on your collage to suggest a choice between two sides.

4 Harvest four to six words from your scrap paper, and form a sentence or add some other element by hand to further develop ideas of walking the line.

Build Slowly

Maybe you run. Maybe you used to run. Maybe you wish you could run. Maybe you are grateful that you don't run. Regardless, the lessons from running can be applied to anything. Substitute your favorite athletic or art activity for the running-related words:

- Warm up.
- Training is not just for the body, but also for the mind.
- To run a marathon you must start at the beginning and build slowly.

The text here comes from an article about the crane pose in yoga. The fork-and-spoon couple is the focal point of this composition.

PROMPT

When making a collage with multiple colors, textures, and patterns, lay out your papers first before committing to the design by gluing them in place.

1   Overwhelm your page with color, texture, and pattern. Build slowly by "painting" your background with papers and matte medium.

2   Balance the colorful background with simple lines and an element that will frame your focal point.

3   Add a focal point.

AMY DUNCAN

Accept Solitude

Solitude, silence, loneliness. It's easy to conflate one with the other. Solitude can quickly slide into loneliness. Silence can support one and cause the other. The capacity to find flow and ease with oneself and one's pursuits is the pureness of solitude, the pleasure that comes from quiet time on one's own. When doubt enters, the pleasure of one becomes the nightmare of the other. Accept solitude without fear of what it might reveal.

A moment's solitude is precious. So is the mind that can accept it.

PROMPT

1 Create a sense of depth by placing dark values in the background and light values in the foreground.

2 Create a silhouette using one of your stencils.

3 Overlap the silhouette onto your depth-filled composition.

Wait without Thought

Throughout life you probably have had to wait for some kind of news, such as a medical test result, a decision about a job offer, the birth of a child of a friend or relative, or countless other things. As you wait, you may want to put yourself into a hopeful frame of mind. It's easy to let the imagination run free with thoughts of what *might* happen.

Instead, try to wait without thought and focus on the present moment. Maybe that manifests itself by listening to the inhale and exhale of your breath. Or perhaps it is a methodical way of punching circles into a piece of paper for a project—or slicing carrots. Whatever you do, resolve to be fully present in each and every action.

PROMPT

1   Prepare pieces of collage paper by methodically punching or drawing circles, cutting strips, or repeating another kind of action.

2   Build a two- or three-layer collage with variations of one color.

3   Add a focal point and any other additional texture to tell a story.

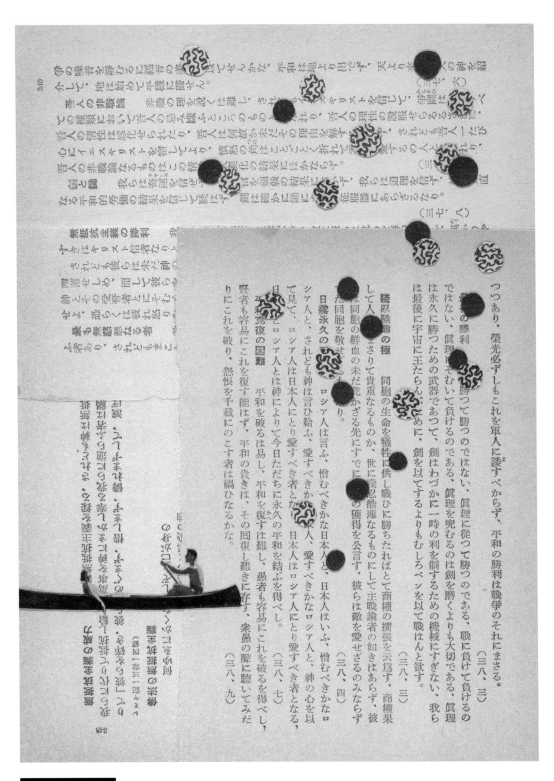

BRENDA ROSE

Only Connect

When making art with a particular theme, it helps to dive into the etymology of a word. Choose a word, look at its origins, synonyms, and antonyms, and ask "How do I connect to it?" As an example, let's look at the word *conceive*. Some synonyms for conceive include "to imagine," "to picture," "to think of," and, of course, "to become pregnant." From there, new thoughts arise, such as "What was conceived must be birthed."

The womb can represent a nest and an incubator for creative ideas, not just babies. I embody this in my work through bird imagery because birds not only hatch *from* eggs but also lay and incubate eggs.

PROMPT

1 Examine your work. What themes do you see? Distill them down to a couple of words.

2 Look up the etymology of those words. Let this discovery direct your next composition.

JOHANNA GOODMAN

Wilderness Mindset

The wilderness mindset understands that there are many paths to the same destination, both literally and figuratively. Some are direct, others are circuitous. Some intentionally avoid obstacles. All require balance between attention within and attention without along the path. When you acknowledge a wilderness mindset, you also accept being present to the unpredictability of life. How can you apply a wilderness mindset to your own work?

PROMPT

1 Begin by creating a background, whatever you like.

2 Add an unusual creature or unexpected animal imagery to your collage as a nod to the unpredictability of life.

VADIM SOLOVYEV

Send Some Mail

What makes a good mail day for you? Receiving a package? A personal letter? A special card? What about receiving mail art?

In the 1960s, artists began sending postcards, letters, and objects covered in drawings and text through the postal service. It sure feels great to get one of these creations in the mail, and they are fun to make, too! These small-scale artworks move through the hands of countless people and are designed to be seen by everyone who touches them. Some artists feel that the marks, wear, and interaction with others that happen along the way from sender to receiver complete the work.

Collage adapts perfectly to this process. Anyone can do it. It can become a focused practice, as described here by artist Karen Arp-Sandel, or a one-off that you do from time to time.

ARTIST STATEMENT
Karen Arp-Sandel

"In 2007, I began a collage postcard exchange across the state line between New York and Massachusetts with my collage student and dear friend Suzi Banks Baum (see page 104). After 1,000 days of correspondence, we curated our first exhibition and named our process FeMail.

As you might guess, FeMail is mail art by females. It represents our authentic feminine voices. It captures the struggles and joys of the working woman, motherhood, and the universal female experience. Through visual dialogue, the postcards take us on a journey to places, life events, milestones, and spiritual inquiry. The written word is included as a graphic element, as poetry and quotation, and as affectionate notes.

Over the years FeMail has become a mail art community without borders. FeMail is created using scissors, glue, paper, and postcards. Art is not separate from life; rather, it is a way of life. Anyone can do it."

OLD SOUTH CHURCH, BOSTON, MASS.

PROMPT

1 Find a substrate thick enough for mail art, such as an old postcard, a box, or really anything that has a bit of weight.

2 Gather 5–10 pieces of paper with text, patterns, images, or whatever appeals to you. Don't think; respond intuitively.

3 Play with the layout of these papers on both the front and back of the substrate.

4 Leave space for the address—and consider how the stamp becomes part of the composition, too.

Find Kindness

Scan through your body. Observe any tension or tightness. Bring focus to those areas, then imagine space being created around them. Notice the tension; say hello to it. Send the tightness some kindness. Speak to it. Imagine the words you would say to a beloved friend, child, or parent if they expressed the same kind of tension or tightness. Can you picture that language expanding to include yourself? Say to yourself what you would say to others.

LINDEN ELLER

PROMPT

1   Establish a background layer that uses a textured or colored paper.

2   Layer on top with transparent papers. As you layer them, the transparent papers will obscure some areas more than others. Let this layering be a metaphor for the tightness and tension that you may carry in your body but don't acknowledge.

3   Add text and stencils or cutouts to represent how you might visually convey the act of treating yourself with kindness.

Make the Most of Boredom

When you're stuck in a long checkout line, take advantage of the chance to do nothing, be present, and observe your environment. The best ideas can bubble up when you don't have to focus on something specific. Relax into it, and just **BE**.

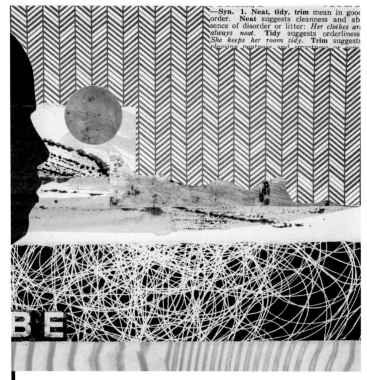

This collage features a silhouette eyeing a green circle and a green landscape-like mix of papers. While the focal point is on the edge of the composition, the line of the landscape keeps the eye moving.

PROMPT

1   Combine two to four very different visual textures, using only black, white, and two additional colors. Bonus if your colors are sort of complementary.

2   Add a focal point. Your focal point can be centered, off-centered, on the edge, in the thirds, or wherever you want it. Choose something that keeps the eye moving through your composition.

Come Alive

"How are you?"

"Busy."

Countless people utter this call and response daily. You may have said these words as you examine your calendar, filled with welcomed and unwelcomed obligations, chores, and engagements. Life throws unexpected curveballs that will force you to say no to some opportunities, parties, and gatherings. When this happens, what really matters still finds a way into your life. To choose to say no on your own takes courage. When you do, be ready to come alive.

PROMPT

1 Plan to create a collage with black and white papers plus one other color.

2 Look through your collection of text. Choose a phrase or make a phrase from a series of words that represents aliveness to you. Consider the color and the size of the letters. Let this direct your collage.

3 Build your collage to include a focal point and elements that appear to be in conversation with each other either literally or figuratively.

4 Add your text as the last or one of the last layers of your collage.

Tap the Power of Enthusiasm

Straight-up enthusiasm does a lot—often more than external motivation does—to carry you through challenging tasks and opportunities. Enthusiasm is not something you can fake or conjure. Try to figure out what turns you on and pursue that as an avenue toward the "Aha!" moment of transformation.

Find the new text you want, then connect it and frame it. The use of gesso here makes a more neutral background.

PROMPT

1. Redact a piece of found text into something new. You can transform text through redaction in different ways. Use a marker to block out text; circle words you like, and crosshatch the rest away; use color, such as with a highlighter, to make new meaning. Or combine techniques. For example, you could circle words, then highlight them with watercolor or another color medium. Highlight or transform the text to reflect something about which you're especially enthusiastic.

2. Layer that with other collage imagery and color, but limit your color palette. Use three colors at most.

Focus on What Is Right

It's really easy to get caught up in daily frustrations or to focus on the thing you wished you had done differently: failing to reach out to someone in need, exposing yourself to a new situation, or a myriad of other things. In these moments it might be especially helpful to pause and examine what is right in your life, while still not ignoring the frustrations. Can you recognize what each may be offering you? You might learn what you need to do, what you need to let go of, what you need to change, or what you need to just let be in your life.

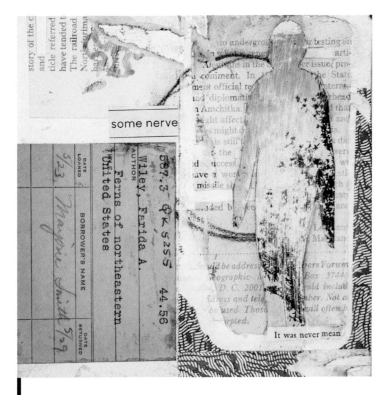

some nerve

It was never mean

PROMPT

1 Go into your paper recycling bag. Tear a random page out of a magazine, and grab an envelope with a window and two other unusual pieces of paper. (Remember that interior envelope patterns vary widely and are great material for collages. You may want to start saving them if you don't already.)

2 Read through the text on the papers, then cut out two or three strings of words representing what is right in your life or reminding you to pause.

3 Combine it all together.

This collage uses two pieces of added text: *some nerve* and *It was never mean*. The juxtaposition of the statements serves as a reminder when you get worked into a tizzy to pause, observe, and focus on what is right in your life.

Love Everything That Gets in Your Way

Teachers are everywhere. They exist in the long checkout line at the grocery store, in the person driving slowly, in the bored and lonely feelings. Whatever the obstacle is, it wants to teach you something. Be present to it. These obstacles help you grow. They become catalysts for awakening and change.

Rather than pushing away the hard things, allow feelings and sensations, both good and bad, to arise in you. When you stop struggling against your honest emotions (especially if they are negative), you will stop being defined by them. The best fuel for transformation is letting yourself feel what you need to feel. Then you can choose your next steps.

Using a packing tape transfer instead of glue to add the ballerina lets the yellow show through her body, so she's integrated into the composition more completely.

PROMPT

1 Pick the smallest pieces you can find out of your collage scraps. Organize them on your collage substrate, maybe by color or perhaps by shape. Play around with the scraps for some time before committing to a design. When I do this, I often have a second collage going at the same time, so I work on that one for a while before returning to my original piece. What works for one might not work for the other.

2 Once you have a composition you like, glue it all down. Admire your work.

3 Add a packing tape transfer.

Delve into the Dark Nights of the Soul

Life challenges all of us. Sometimes these challenges loom over us and push us into a dark space. Other times those challenges pick, pick, pick away at our fiber, inciting us to change, to step out of an old story or an old way of being and into a new way of being. Start with those challenges: How does your soul wander into their dark corners? What might be a first step away from what looms over you and toward something new? Maybe it's an action in your art-making or something in your day-to-day living. Try giving yourself restrictions to break you out of old habits.

GINGER SEDLAROVA

PROMPT

1 Begin with a highly patterned piece of paper as your first layer. Mute it with gesso if you have it, or just leave the paper as is.

2 Select another piece of paper that has interesting yet contrasting texture and randomly cut it into two or three pieces. Reassemble these pieces over your first layer, letting a bit of the first layer peek through. Let the layer that peeks through represent the part of you that wants to step into newness.

3 Add a third layer, with a focal point. Trace a handmade or purchased stencil with an ebony pencil or other soft pencil. Paint inside the outlines with gesso.

4 Add a fourth layer. It can be something such as dotted lines, harvested text, or something else. You decide.

Reframe Negativity

We all want to know how we can contribute to and make a difference in our communities. Pursuing creative projects sometimes can feel as though it doesn't matter in the face of big global problems such as injustice and inequality. In fact, art and poetry can be some of the most useful ways to express the impact of global problems. Not only can they provide the maker with a way to advocate for the self and others, they also can provide the viewer with peace and comfort.

MAKING WAVES

In this image, the floor has been removed. As a result, two people are looking out into an open space in a building that is now filled with the sky and a mountain. By adding the bird sitting on the railing and the words "making waves," the composition is completely reframed.

PROMPT

1 Find a magazine image that has a window, door, or some other shape that can be removed. Cut out an opening.

2 Position the magazine image over another image. Make sure to consider paradox and juxtaposition.

3 Add two or more other elements.

Show Up and Get to Work

Do you ever wait for the lightning bolt of inspiration to strike, for a challenge to ease, or for something to land in your path telling you what to do next? Often the best way to coax out inspiration is to ignore the desire to wait, and just start. As artist Chuck Close said, "Inspiration is for amateurs—the rest of us just show up and get to work."

MAKE EVERYDAY SPARKLE™

Using gesso as a masking tool is a good way to transform a collage, drawing, or painting. When diluted with a little bit of water, gesso can neutralize a busy background. You can also layer it over a collage or painting and then sand away portions of it to reveal lower layers.

PROMPT

1   Collect images with strong outlines and shapes. Collage them onto a base layer.

2   Use gesso or another kind of white paint mixed with a little water and paint over the collage. Wipe off the excess with a rag, then let the collage dry.

3   Sand with a fine sandpaper to reveal some of the textures and color from the original base layer.

4   Add other black-and-white elements, including text, collage, pen and ink, or something else.

Let the Light Shift

Sometimes a task feels larger than life or too big to accomplish, and we make it even bigger by thinking about it and overthinking it. Then somehow the light shifts, changing our perspective, and all of a sudden we grow in determination and efficiency, and all is well.

GUILLAUME CHIRON

PROMPT

1. Choose a background that fools with perspective. Look for a vanishing point, a horizon line, or the corner of a room.

2. Play with scale. Use two items that when paired together causes one of them to appear unusually large or small.

3. Add some other elements. So many options!

In this piece red dots link an oversized bird with a human figure, solidifying the connection between the two subjects of the composition. You could create this connection with other papers, stamps, or text.

Follow Your Intuition

When we follow our intuition, it often feels like a smashing and colliding of elements into something great and wonderful. It can also be puzzlelike, layered and filled with microdecisions that require you to trust the process. Collage-making has some of this, too. Choosing, arranging, and layering papers can mirror the microdecisions of the intuitive process. Can you dare to experiment?

Black paper with white swirls serves as the background for this collage, with four strips from green and black paper connecting the background pieces. Made with commercial punches, the bird and the circle form the focal point.

PROMPT

1 Cut a patterned paper in half. Glue each half to one side of your collage substrate.

2 With contrasting papers, reconnect the split. Choose colors that link to the first patterned paper.

3 Add a focal point, such as a strong shape off-centered, multiple shapes or forms on the diagonal, or a combination of the two.

Work Expands to Fill the Time

"Work expands to fill the time" is a proverb coined by the twentieth-century British scholar C. Northcote Parkinson. You can use this saying to your advantage by scheduling blocks of time and giving yourself time limits.

At the start of your work session, try setting a time limit with the goal of completing your collage within that period. Or if you can't find the right paper or you are unsure about a compositional layout, give yourself a specified amount of time to waffle between ideas. Just make sure when the time is up, you either make a decision or stop!

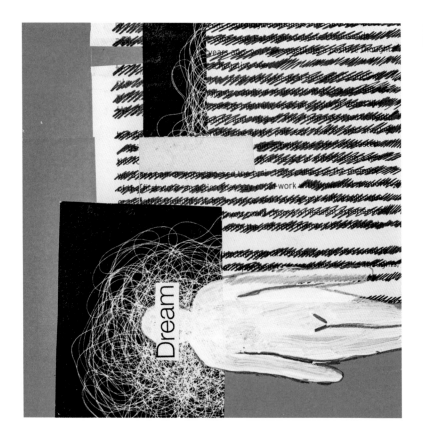

PROMPT

1 Limit the amount of time you dedicate to finding a shape you like in a magazine. Set a timer, then start harvesting an image. Finish when the timer goes off.

2 Using stencil material, if you have it, or an old file folder, create a stencil from the shape.

3 Make a background out of scraps from past collages.

4 Cut out your stencil shape from patterned paper, or draw or paint the outline of your stencil onto your collage. Add defining lines if appropriate.

5 Harvest some words out of your text paper to link the stenciled image together with the rest of the composition.

Create Accountability

You may find that you need something outside of yourself to keep you accountable to the artistic practice you are trying to build. Perhaps you make a weekly date with a friend where you each pursue your own creative practice side by side. You can do this in person or in an online meeting. Other options include joining online daily challenges or groups dedicated to creative practice or committing to posting to your own social media or blog.

#THE100 DAYPROJECT

#The100DayProject is a free, global art project that takes place every year. The idea, started by Lindsay Jean Thomson, is simple: Pick an action, do it every day, and document and share your process online. Artists, creatives, and makers doing #The100DayProject can choose any medium or art form. Two artists working with paper and collage who completed #The100DayProject challenge in 2020 are e bond and Laura Didyk. Here is more about their work, in their own words.

PROMPT

Search #The100DayProject on Instagram for inspiration and to follow projects. Then, join #The100DayProject and share your work with that hashtag and #CollageYourLife.

ARTIST STATEMENT
e bond

"#100MapsToAnywhere started as a daily project to explore both the idea and form of maps to document nonphysical spaces, emotions, natural occurrences, and time. Working with a single idea in very small ways, every day over an extended period of time, allows me to delve deeper into a concept. It also gives space for multiple ways of seeing the same idea. Since the daily maps project began, these ideas and images have permeated all of my thinking, from my personal daily sketchbooks to my larger professional work."

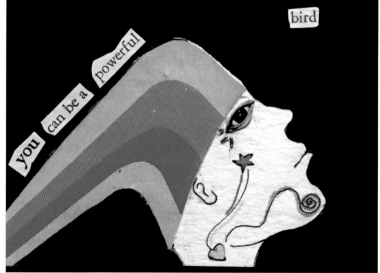

ARTIST STATEMENT

Laura Didyk

"#Lauras100DaysOfSmallDrawings was inspired by my love of working small—in this case, with playing card–size pieces of watercolor paper. After 10 days of drawing flowers, I hit an unexpected wall. Then I loosened up and experimented. I tore and cut paper and words, creating flowers and weather systems, and incorporated text into collages of creatures and characters. Over time, these multimedia poems grew in depth and complexity, begged for even more freedom and abstraction. Arms, legs, and hair stretched and spilled beyond the confines of the paper as I moved into more challenging, more rewarding, and more delightful territory."

Idea-Generating Cards

IF YOU SIT DOWN TO CREATE AND NOTHING COMES, try using source materials such as a reflective reading, images, an object right in front of you, or some other prompt. One good way to begin is to make yourself a deck of idea-generating cards. Think flash cards for creativity. They hold prompts and provocations, challenges and ideas for making and creating.

To make your own cards, begin with broad categories, such as "the five senses," "motion," or "abstract words." Seven or eight categories is plenty. For each category, list 12 to 15 words or prompts. You can start with a memory, a concept, or really anything you'd like to explore more deeply. Tailor your lists to reflect the themes you are most interested in. Continue adding words to your lists over a couple of days, then pare down your complete list to 100 prompts.

I've included some of my own lists to get you started. Many of these relate to prompts and techniques from this book. Write them down on slips of paper, place them in a jar, a box, or a bag. And then the next time you feel "stuck," draw one out and make something!

MEDIUM AND TECHNIQUE

- Play with pencil.
- Use found materials.
- Repurpose old artwork by painting on it.
- Add embroidery.
- Tear and visually stitch back together.
- Create a stencil from a magazine image.
- Make a stamp for a focal point.
- Incorporate torn paper edges.
- Get dimensional; add objects.
- Use a packing tape transfer.
- Add paint, gesso, or inks.

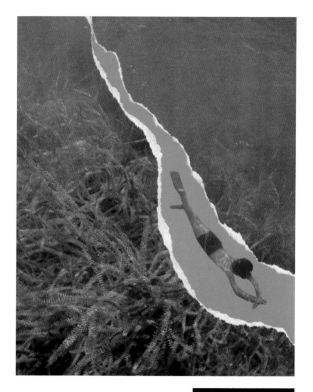

LAURA WEILER

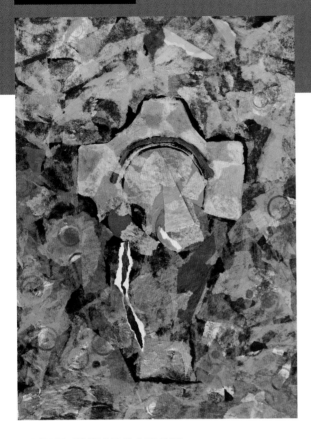

PAPER EXPLORATION

- Paint with papers; make a landscape of the view outside your window, your favorite spot, or anywhere else.
- Paint with papers; make a portrait of yourself, your pet, your best friend, or anyone else.
- Pair different kinds of papers together.
- Use ephemera from your day-to-day.
- Create on a shipping label or other unusual substrate.
- Incorporate vintage papers.
- Use a specific issue of a magazine.
- Integrate a map.
- Use transparent layers: old sewing patterns, vellum, transparencies.
- Cut an old artwork into strips and weave the strips together.

ELEMENTS & PRINCIPLES OF DESIGN

- Explore physical textures by adding fabric, wool, or felt.
- Play with textured images.
- Employ implied line.
- Get bold with color.
- Go for high contrast.
- Explore complementary color.
- Use only analogous colors.
- Use your favorite color.
- Explore common color associations:
  - Red: anger, love, courage, valor, hot, revolution, siren, power, passion
  - Orange: communication, warm, glowing, energetic, rambunctious, earth, autumn

continued on next page

ELEMENTS & PRINCIPLES
OF DESIGN *continued*

- Yellow: sun, newness, hope, happiness, good cheer, friendly, optimism
- Green: fertility, fresh, nature, environment, spring, slimy, jealousy, folklore
- Blue: sky, water, serenity, cool, meditative, devotion
- Purple: royalty, dignity, dynamic, grandeur, mysterious
- Black: practical, glamorous, sleek, stealthy, empowering, authority, strength, debt-free
- White: simplicity, virginal, clarity, pristine, weightless, innocence
- Incorporate a pattern.
- Play with repetition.
- Use paradox.
- Simplify: Use no more than four pieces of paper.
- Pair together opposites.
- Explore mood.
- Use typography as image.

MOMENTOUS MOMENTS

- Dream of a wedding, real or imagined.
- Welcome a baby.
- Depict a birthday.
- Document a child's milestones.
- Honor a loved one who has passed.
- Celebrate a promotion.
- Examine a failure.
- Use ephemera from travel.

NARRATIVE

- Tell a story about your past.
- Tell a story about your future.
- Invent an animal or creature, and place it in unique settings.
- Put someone on a quest.
- Weave in a piece of history.
- Explore myths and folktales.
- Comment on the news of the day.

JULIA NALA

JACK FELICE

PORTRAITS

- Self-portrait
- Self-portrait that doesn't include the human figure
- Portrait of a family member
- Portrait of a friend
- Portrait of a pet
- Portrait of an enemy
- A figure from imagination
- Animals
- Sinister creatures
- Benevolent friend
- Play with biography and autobiography.

CONCEPTUAL & COMPOSITIONAL

- Landscape
- Cityscape
- Moonscape
- Other kinds of -scape
- Fantasy
- Place something out of context.
- Make your own rule.
- Abstract
- Embrace chaos.
- Noir
- Visual puns
- Mix meaning.
- Mix metaphors.
- Mix time periods.
- Reframe or recontextualize.
- Express cultural origin.
- Merge figures together.
- Play with the power of suggestion.
- Use irony.
- Flora and fauna
- Use humor.
- Parody
- Nostalgia
- Appropriate a material or idea, and make it your own.
- Play with juxtaposition.

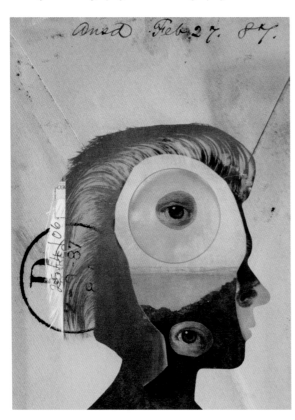

SARAH JARRETT

chapter

4

Create the Container

OLLAGES CAN BE CREATED flat on cardboard or paper substrates or on pages of books you've made. You can also first make a collage and then add it to a book later. In this chapter I'll show you how to construct a few different kinds of handmade books.

When you drink from the river of silence
shall you indeed sing. And when you have
reached the mountaintop, then you shall
begin to climb. And when the earth shall
claim your limbs, then shall you truly
dance.

Kahlil Gibran - The Prophet

Making Your Own Collage Books

Handmade books give designated space for your collage practice.
Sure, you can make a collage on any substrate, but a book keeps many of
your collages together in one place. You can slip small books into a bag
or a pocket so they're available on the go. No matter what size book you
make, it will serve as a container for your collages and, over time, become
a place that showcases this practice you are developing.

A Note about Paper Grain

Most papers have a grain, or a direction in which the fibers run. Paper folds easiest when it is folded *with* the grain. As you dive into making books, pay attention to the grain of your paper. You want it to run parallel to the spine of your book. It's not the end of the world if it runs in the other direction, but you'll end up with a sturdier book and with pages that fold more readily if the grain is parallel to the spine. This orientation allows the paper to swell or expand if exposed to moisture without damaging the binding of the book.

To check which direction the paper grain is running, lightly fold (do not crease!) the paper parallel to the short edge and then parallel to the long edge. Whichever way the paper wants to fold more easily is the direction of the grain. In most commercial papers, the grain is parallel to the long edge of the paper. If the grain is parallel to the shortest side of the paper, it is called *grain short*.

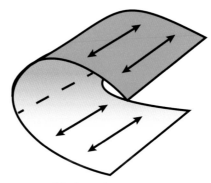

with the grain

against the grain

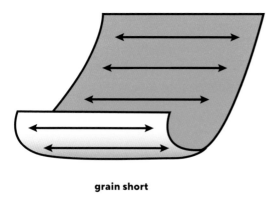

grain short

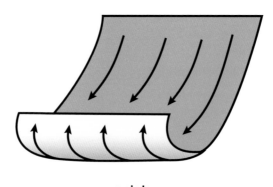

grain long

Rejuvenated Cardboard Box Book

You can make this book with materials you find or with materials you buy. You can make it any size, either square or rectangular, and with either blank or printed pages. Try using museum brochures as pages and then collage right over the content.

TOOLS AND MATERIALS

- **Paper for interior pages**
- **Bone folder**
- **Piece of newsprint or other blank paper 2" wide and as tall as your desired interior page height**
- **Ceramic pin tool or awl**
- **Funky cardboard boxes or any kind of sturdy cardboard for covers**
- **Thin cardboard for spine strip (Cereal boxes work well.)**
- **Brown paper packing tape, duct tape, or cloth tape, 2"–3" wide**
- **Bookbinding needle**
- **Waxed-linen thread or dental floss**

PROCESS

1 Fold a sheet of interior page paper in half parallel to the grain, using a bone folder to make the crease. This creates a *folio* (1A). Repeat with additional sheets to create three to six folios. Nestle the folios together to form a *signature*, the bookbinding term referring to a unit of sheets that are folded and stitched together. (How many sheets you put in each signature will depend on the thickness of the paper you're using.) Repeat five times so you have six signatures total (1B).

2 Make a jig, or pattern, for punching holes in the six signatures along the folded line. With the 2"-wide newsprint in a portrait orientation, fold it in half lengthwise. Open it up, and punch one hole about 1" in from the top edge (hole A) and another hole about 1" in from the bottom edge (hole B).

　Fold the newsprint in half short edge to short edge and open it back up. Using the ceramic pin tool or an awl, punch one hole about 1" above this fold line (hole C) and another hole about 1" below this fold line (hole D). Your completed jig should have four holes lined up along the center of the newsprint.

3 Place the jig into one signature. Use an awl to punch holes all the way through the pages in that signature. Repeat for each signature.

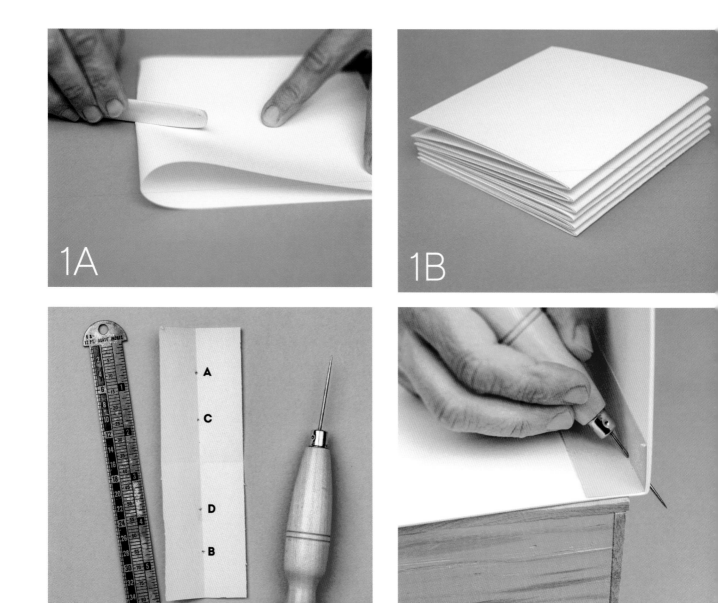

continued on next page

Rejuvenated Cardboard Box Book *continued*

4 Cut two cover boards ⅛" larger than your folded interior pages.

5 Cut a piece of thin cardboard the same height as your cover boards for the spine strip. To determine the width of the spine, stack all your signatures together and measure their width. It should be around 1" when the signatures are not compressed. The spine should be wide enough to allow the pages to expand when you add collage material. A good rule of thumb is to at most double the compressed measurement of all the signatures. If you know you will use thick papers in your collages, allow even more width for the spine.

6 Cut a piece of tape twice as long as the spine plus 2". Center the spine in the horizontal middle of the tape. Place the cardboard covers about ⅛" away from the spine.

7 Pull the tape up from both the top and bottom to secure the spine strip between the two covers. Use the bone folder to firmly press the tape in place.

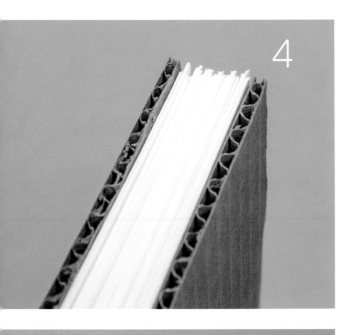

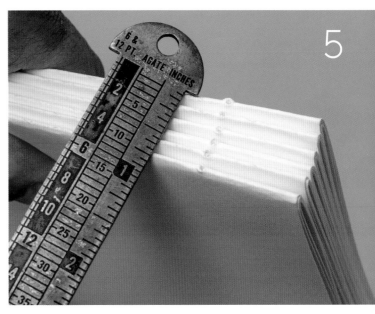

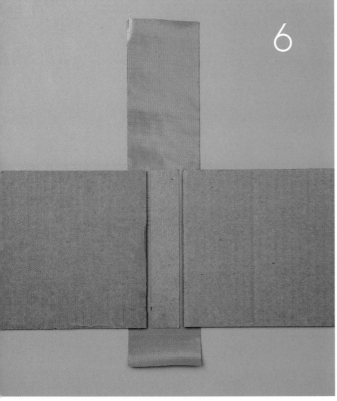

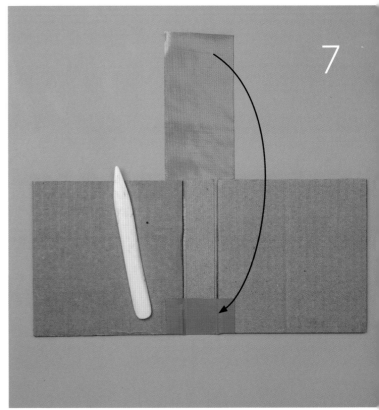

continued on next page

Rejuvenated Cardboard Box Book **189**

8A

Rejuvenated Cardboard Box Book *continued*

8 Transfer onto the inside of the cardboard spine the hole marks from the newsprint jig that you made in step 2. Parallel to each hole from the jig, mark six small dots across the spine (A). These mark each place where your needle will stitch the signatures into the spine. Using the awl, punch a hole in each mark all the way through the spine (B).

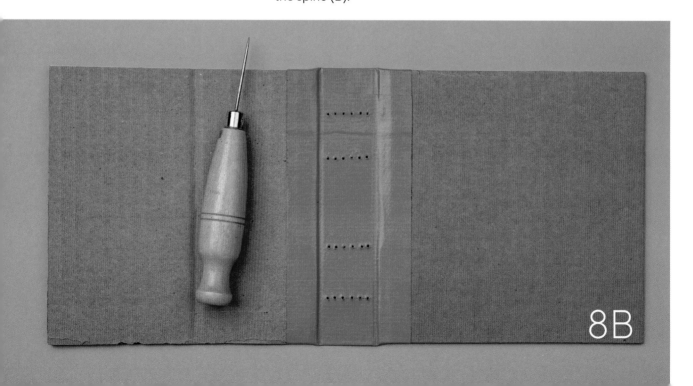

8B

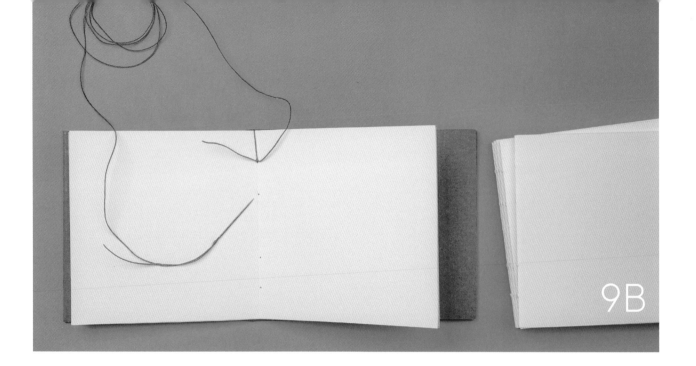

9B

9 Using a bookbinding needle and waxed-linen thread, sew the signatures into the spine as follows:

A Beginning on the inside of signature #1, pull the needle and most of the thread out through the top hole in the spine, leaving a tail about 2"–3" long in the middle of the signature. Wrap the needle and working thread around the top of the spine and back into the same signature.

B Tie the tail from step A into a knot as close as possible to the first binding hole, as shown in the photo above.

C Pull the needle and thread out through the second hole and to the outside of the spine.

D Poke the needle through the spine at the third hole and pull the thread through, on the inside of signature #1.

E Bring the needle down to the bottom hole and pull it through the signature and the spine.

F Bring the needle and thread around the bottom of the spine and into signature #1, then pull them back through the bottom hole of the signature only. (Do not bring the needle through the bottom hole of the spine at this point; the needle should be in between the spine and the signature.)

continued on next page

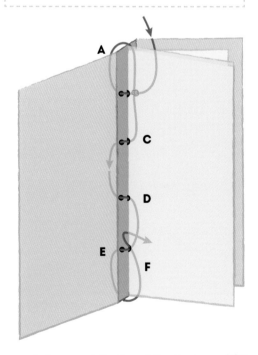

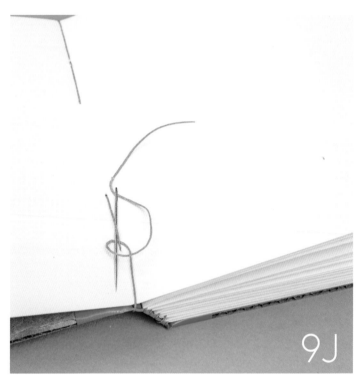

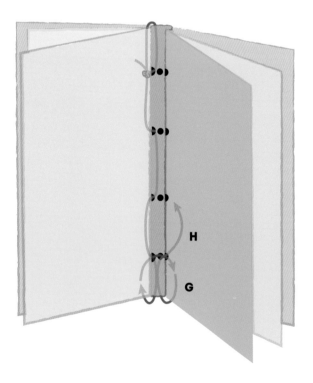

G Add a new signature and, working from the outside of the signature to the inside, pull the needle and thread through the bottom hole of the signature only. (Do not bring the needle through the spine at this point.) You are now on the inside of signature #2.

H Bring the needle around the bottom of the signature and through the bottom hole on the spine, then back into the **SAME** hole of the second signature. Continue sewing up the signature, using the same pattern established in the first signature.

I Repeat steps C–H until all six of the signatures are sewn into the book.

J To finish, tie off your thread on the inside of the last section.

Now you are ready to add in collages.

Simple Accordion Book

Accordion books are easy to create and fun to fill with collages. Make individual collages or build across the page spread to create a longer, continuous work of art. Accordions can be any size. As you practice and become more familiar with the technique, play around with size and shape to find what you prefer.

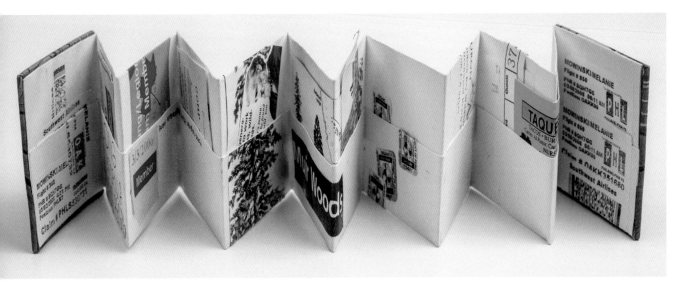

TOOLS AND MATERIALS

- **Strip of paper, ideally grain short**
- **Bone folder**

Accordion books are made from two types of folds: mountain folds and valley folds.

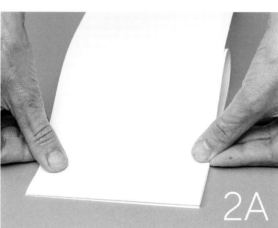

PROCESS

1 Fold the paper in half, and crease with your bone folder.

2 Open the paper, and admire your mountain fold. Bring the mountain fold toward the top edge of the paper (A), and crease with your bone folder. Then fold the other edge of the paper up to meet your mountain fold (B), and crease with the bone folder.

continued on next page

Simple Accordion Book *continued*

3 Unfold. Reverse the valley folds. All the folds should now point up in the same direction, creating a soft wave.

4 Fold each mountain toward the top edge of the paper. Use your bone folder to crease each fold in place.

5 Fold the end of the paper up to meet your mountain folds, and crease with the bone folder.

6 Repeat steps 3–5 until you are satisfied with the width of each accordion page.

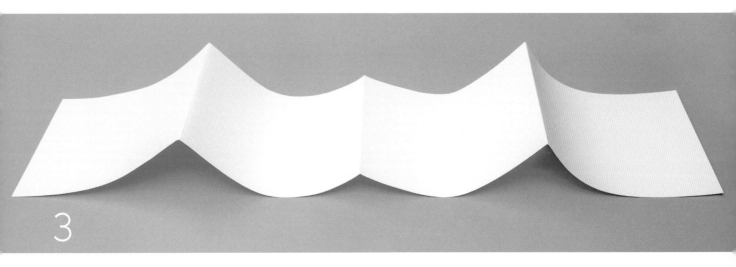

3

4

5

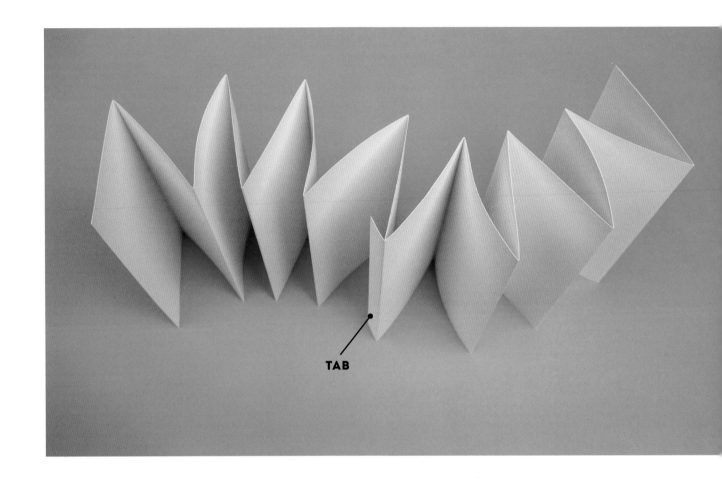

TAB

NOT BIG ENOUGH?

If your folded strip isn't long enough for your purposes, you can extend it by attaching it to another folded strip. To do this, convert one folded end of an accordion strip into a tab by trimming that panel down to ½", then adhering it to another folded accordion strip with glue or double-stick tape. Make sure you continue the mountain and valley fold pattern you started with, by flipping over the new strip if need be.

Storage Book

Storage books can be used to frame multiple collages, portions of collages, or other items. Once you are familiar with the structure, experiment with cutouts of different shapes and sizes. Hedi Kyle, my bookbinding mentor and instructor in graduate school, introduced me to this structure.

TOOLS AND MATERIALS

- **Five 8" × 10" sheets card stock (grain short) for pages and cover**
- **Strip of Tyvek for accordion spine (height of the folded card stock × 8")**
- **Double-stick tape (¼"–½" wide)**
- **Bone folder**
- **Awl**
- **Ruler**
- **Craft knife**
- **Cutting mat**

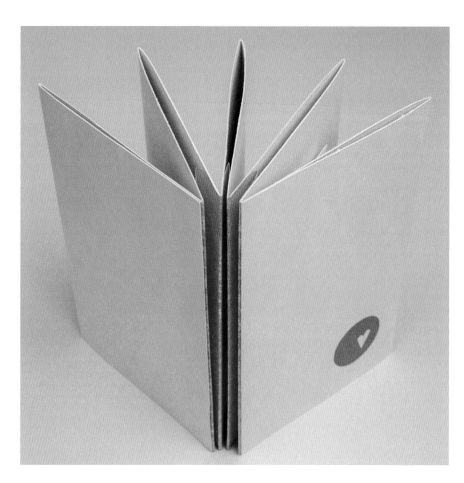

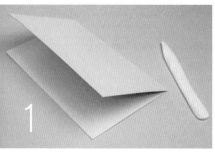

PROCESS
Prepare Pages and Accordion

1 Fold each sheet of card stock in half in the direction of the grain. The fold in the card stock will be positioned along the open edge of the book, while the open edge of the card stock will be positioned along the spine edge of the book.

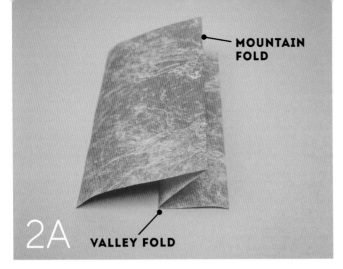

MOUNTAIN FOLD

2A

VALLEY FOLD

2B

2C

2D

2 Position the Tyvek strip with the side you want showing on your final spine faceup. Fold the Tyvek into an accordion as follows:

A Fold the strip in half lengthwise, then open, and bring the center mountain fold toward one outside edge of the paper. Crease, making a valley fold.

B Bring the opposite edge of the paper up to the center mountain fold, and crease, creating a second valley fold.

C Open the Tyvek, turn it over, and reverse the center valley fold. You should now have three mountain folds faceup. Fold each mountain toward one unfolded edge of the Tyvek, creasing each new valley fold as you make it. Fold the end of the paper to meet the other mountain folds, creasing to make the last valley fold.

NOTE: The accordion will be the spine of the book. Eventually each of the pages will be adhered to it.

D You will end with the inside of the Tyvek strip faceup, with three mountain folds and four valley folds.

continued on next page

Storage Book *continued*

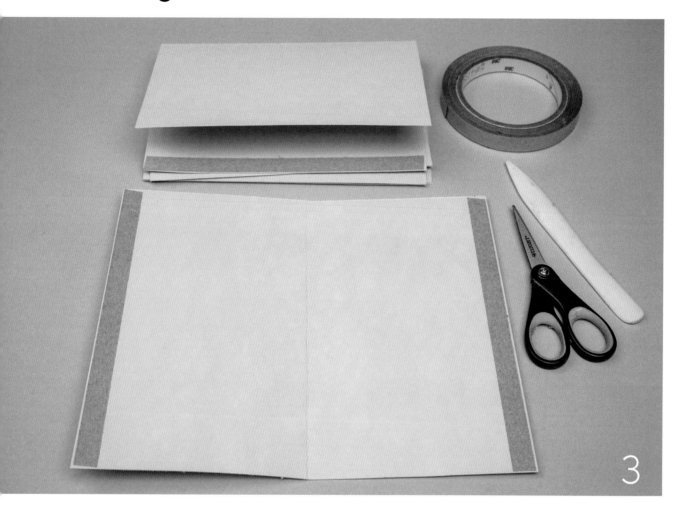

3   Place a strip of double-stick tape along each inside open edge, or the spine edge, of the card stock.

4   Designate two pages for the cover, and set aside. With the remaining four pages, create any of the storage styles described below.

STORAGE STYLES

On the following pages, I describe three styles of storage pages: collage insert, frame, and pocket. Experiment with placement, size, and scale as you practice these methods.

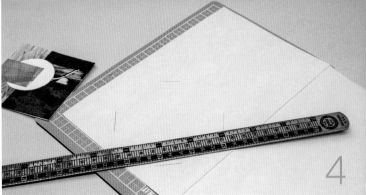

Collage Insert

1 Open one page, and place it on a cutting mat.

2 Place the collage to be inserted on top of the left side of the page. Decide which corners of your collage you will tuck into the page. Tucking in all four corners will provide the most security for your collage, but you may want to tuck in only two or three corners depending on your composition.

3 With an awl, mark at a 45-degree angle on the book page about ½" above where each collage corner will be inserted (eight holes total). The holes serve as stopping points for your knife. Without them, it's easy to make your cuts much longer than desired. Remove the collage that will be inserted.

4 Using a straightedge, cut slits from dot to dot at each corner.

5 Slide each corner of the collage into the slits.

Frame

1 On the inside left or right of one of the pages, trace around the collage to be framed. Set aside the collage for a moment.

2 Cut a frame ⅛"–¼" inside your tracing using a craft knife, ruler, and cutting mat.

3 Apply double-stick tape around the edge of the frame on the back of the card stock.

4 Remove the tape backing, and attach the collage to the back of the frame. Smooth down the collage with a bone folder.

5 To create a second frame in the same folio, repeat steps 1–4 on the inside of the other folio page, if desired.

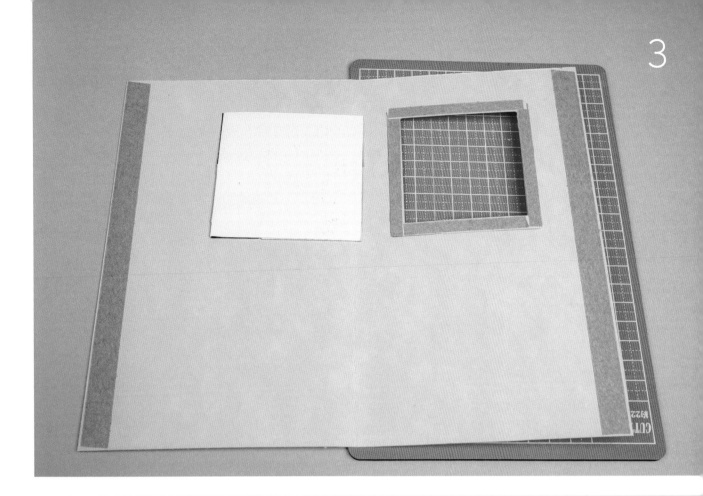

3

4

Pocket

You can make a pocket with any kind of material. Transparent papers allow the viewer to glimpse into the work. Opaque papers hide or suggest the work through windows or openings. Experiment with different types of papers for the individual pages and ways of making openings that reveal the work within.

1 Apply double-stick tape around three edges of the pocket material.

2 Remove the tape backing, and attach the pocket to the page. Smooth down the pocket with a bone folder.

Assembly

1 Determine the order of your inside pages. Lightly number them, or make a mental note of their order. Stack the pages in order, and place them next to the accordion spine.

   NOTE: You will start assembling the book with the last inside page because the cover pages attach in a slightly different way.

2 Open your last book page. Remove the top of the double-stick tape from the inside last page, and attach it to one side of the first mountain fold (A). Smooth down. Repeat on the other side of the first mountain fold, thereby "closing" the page and securing it to the accordion spine (B).

3 Open up your second-to-last page, remove the top of the double-stick tape, and attach it to side one of the second mountain fold. Smooth down. Repeat on the other side of that page. Repeat this step with the rest of the pages.

4 Attach the covers the same way you attached the pages, but note that the cover sheets get adhered to opposites sides of the outer-most valley folds.

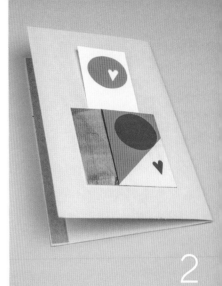

Assembly

2A

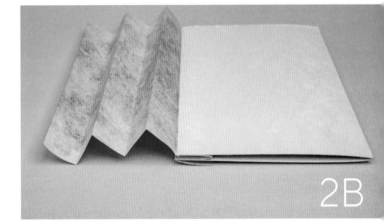

2B

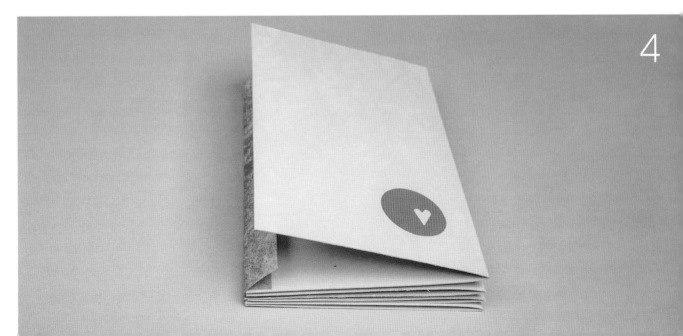

4

Reading List

Creativity

Belsky, Scott. *Making Ideas Happen: Overcoming the Obstacles Between Vision and Reality.* Portfolio, 2012.

Cameron, Julia. *The Artist's Way: A Spiritual Path to Higher Creativity,* 25th anniversary edition. TarcherPerigee, 2016.

Csikszentmihalyi, Mihaly. *Creativity: Flow and the Psychology of Discovery and Invention.* Harper Perennial, 2013.

Gilbert, Elizabeth. *Big Magic: Creative Living Beyond Fear.* Riverhead Books, 2016.

Goldberg, Natalie. *Writing Down the Bones: Freeing the Writer Within,* 30th anniversary edition. Shambhala, 2016.

Greenhalgh, Wendy Ann. *Stop Look Breathe Create.* Ilex, 2017.

Hinchcliff, Jennie, and Carolee Gilligan Wheeler. *Good Mail Day: A Primer for Making Eye-Popping Postal Art.* Quarry Books, 2009.

Young, James Webb. *A Technique for Producing Ideas.* CreateSpace, 2015.

Artists and Daily Practice

Bayles, David, and Ted Orland. *Art & Fear: Observations on the Perils (and Rewards) of Artmaking.* Image Continuum Press, 2001.

Bennett, Cat. *Making Art a Practice: How to Be the Artist You Are.* Findhorn Press, 2013.

Colatosi, Camille. *To Be an Artist: Musicians, Visual Artists, Writers, and Dancers Speak.* E L Kurdyla, 2012.

Currey, Mason. *Daily Rituals: How Artists Work.* Knopf, 2013.

——. *Daily Rituals: Women at Work.* Knopf, 2019.

Duckworth, Angela. *Grit: The Power of Passion and Perseverance.* Scribner, 2016.

Duhigg, Charles. *The Power of Habit: Why We Do What We Do in Life and Business.* Random House, 2014.

Dweck, Carol S. *Mindset: The New Psychology of Success.* Ballantine Books, 2006.

Gladwell, Malcolm. *Outliers: The Story of Success.* Little, Brown and Company, 2008.

Gregory, Danny. *Art Before Breakfast: A Zillion Ways to Be More Creative, No Matter How Busy You Are.* Chronicle Books, 2015.

McGonigal, Kelly. *The Willpower Instinct: How Self-Control Works, Why It Matters, and What You Can Do to Get More of It.* Avery, 2012.

McNiff, Shaun. *Trust the Process: An Artist's Guide to Letting Go.* Shambhala, 1998.

Pink, Daniel H.. *Drive: The Surprising Truth about What Motivates Us.* Riverhead Books, 2009.

Pressfield, Steven. *The War of Art: Break Through the Blocks and Win Your Inner Creative Battles.* Black Irish Entertainment LLC, 2012.

Tharp, Twyla. *The Creative Habit: Learn It and Use It for Life.* Simon & Schuster, 2006.

Tolle, Eckhart. *The Power of Now: A Guide to Spiritual Enlightenment.* Namaste, 2004.

Resources

Materials and Inspiration

International Union of Mail-Artists
https://iuoma-network.ning.com

PaperArts.com
www.paperarts.com

Daniel Smith
https://danielsmith.com

Paper Source
www.papersource.com

StencilGirl Products
www.stencilgirlproducts.com

TALAS
www.talasonline.com

Washi Arts
www.washiarts.com

ONLINE IMAGERY

Creative Commons

https://creativecommons.org

Creative Commons is a nonprofit organization that permits and encourages sharing and reuse of creativity and knowledge. Creative Commons licenses give creators the power to establish how they want other people to share, use, or otherwise enhance a work they have made. This is a great place to look for images that you may use without permission or fear of violating copyright laws.

Library of Congress Prints & Photographs Online Collection

www.loc.gov/pictures

This database includes thousands of images, including artwork (some by well-known artists), maps, architectural plans, and more. Not all of them are copyright free; it is up to the user to determine the appropriate use. Be sure to examine the citation before using.

Pexels

www.pexels.com/public-domain-images

Pexels is a free stock photo and video provider with a section devoted to public domain imagery. There are many other sources like this online. If your vision involves specific images, look for other public domain imagery sites like this one.

Public Domain Vectors

https://publicdomainvectors.org

Line drawings and simplified images make for good packing tape transfers. Public Domain Vectors not only features vintage gems but includes a massive database of other options as well.

Reusable Art

www.reusableart.com

Reusable Art consists of a collection of images that are copyright free and in the public domain in the United States. Most images were chosen from old print materials and range from simple drawings to detailed studies and advertisements.

Wikipedia and Wikimedia Commons

https://en.wikipedia.org/wiki/Wikipedia:Public_domain_image_resources
https://commons.wikimedia.org/wiki/Commons:Free_media_resources/Photography

Both Wikipedia and Wikimedia Commons have comprehensive and extensive lists of sites where you can source public domain media. When using such media, look for the Public Domain Mark that ensures the image is indeed free to use.

WORKSHOP LOCATIONS

Anderson Ranch Arts Center
www.andersonranch.org

Haystack Mountain School of Crafts
www.haystack-mtn.org

Penland School of Craft
https://penland.org

Pyramid Atlantic Art Center
www.pyramidatlanticartcenter.org

Snow Farm
www.snowfarm.org

Women's Studio Workshop
https://wsworkshop.org

Contributors

KAREN ARP-SANDEL creates collage sketchbooks, FeMail mail art, surreal photomontage, painted paper abstracts, found-object assemblage, shard mosaic murals, and hand-bound artist's books. Karen works out of Maison Collage Studio, where she makes art as a daily practice and teaches collage.
https://karenarpsandel.com
@kasart on Instagram

SUZI BANKS BAUM dwells at the crossroad of literary and visual arts. Her collages are entries in her daily creative practice. Suzi teaches online and around the world.
www.suzibanksbaum.com
@suzibb on Instagram

e bond is an artist, writer, bookbinder, educator, and designer. Currently, she makes digital spaces by day and handmade books by night, hangs out with ancient trees on weekends, and writes something close to poems in the spaces between. Under the studio name roughdrAftbooks she creates artist's books, hand-made journals, and mixed-media pieces that blur the boundaries of art, craft, design, and poetry.
https://ebondwork.com
@eisroughdraft on Instagram

KIKE CONGRAINS is a Peruvian artist who founded CollageWave in an effort to popularize collage in Peru. It began as a platform to share collage but has become much more. Now Kike also offers collage workshops to kids in underserved areas, including at rural schools in the jungle. He sees teaching collage to kids as a way to stimulate creativity and, in turn, improve their quality of life.
www.patreon.com/collagewave
@collagewave on Instagram

LAURA DIDYK is a California native who has lived throughout the US. She's been a writer for most of her adult life. In 2014, due to happenstance and heartbreak, Laura started working with found text and ink, and then fell in love with line drawing and collage. She teaches a little, draws a lot, writes some, and does all manner of editing-related work to support her art and writing habits.
www.lauradidyk.com
@lauradidyk on Instagram

AARON GORDON is an analog collage artist from Buffalo, New York, who delved into the world of ruining magazines through his work with a local bookseller. He initially used collage to make flyers for his band, Ghostpool, and has since worked on several projects within the DIY music community.
www.etsy.com/shop/xvcollage
@ctrlx.ctrlv on Instagram

ADAM HUTCHESON didn't tap into his artistic side until his early 30s, at which point a psychic predicted he'd find a creative outlet for some pent-up stress. It came in the form of collage art. He resides in the Philadelphia area, where he juggles two boys and a supportive wife, occasionally finding time to create.
@it_still_moves on Instagram

HEATHER MATTHEW is a paper, print, and book artist who makes work about interconnection between people, nature, and the cosmological world. Heather uses found paper ephemera, handmade paper, and stitching in her daily collages and artworks.
https://heathermatthew.com
@heathermatthewcom on Instagram

Featured Artists

KACI SMITH has a degree in textile design from Moore College of Art and Design and has worked professionally as a handweaver. Although currently working primarily in two-dimensional mixed mediums, Kaci's lifelong passion for pattern, color, and fabric is the endless well of inspiration in her work.
@kacismith on Instagram

EVITA TEZENO creates collages with cubist influences and bold use of color, texture, and shapes. Inspired by images from her childhood, Evita translates these memories through mixed mediums, combining handmade papers, acrylic paints, and found objects.
www.evitatezeno.com
@evitatezeno on Instagram

Simon Blake
www.simonblakestudio.com

Charlota Blunarova
https://blunarova.com

Brandon Brewer
@alltheboystoheart on Instagram

Jacinta Bunnell
www.jacintabunnell.com

Andrés Charbonnier Aunchayna
@charbochayna on Instagram

Guillaume Chiron
https://guillaumechiron.com

Emanuele Crovetto
@emanuelecrovetto on Instagram

Charlotte D'Aigle
www.charlottedaigle.com

Connor "Phib" Dainty
@phibstuff on Instagram

Patricia Doucet
https://patriciadoucet.com

Michelle Dow
@michellehdow on Instagram

Amy Duncan
www.studiofourcorners.com

Linden Eller
www.lindeneller.com

Isabel Espanol
www.isabelespanol.com

Jack Felice
www.jackfelice.com

Ivaldo Ferreira
www.ivaldoferreira.com.br

Ben Lewis Giles
https://benlewisgiles.format.com/

Johanna Goodman
www.johannagoodman.com

Sarah Jarrett
https://sarahjarrettart.com

Colin Johnson
www.colinjohnsonillustration.com

Shraga Kopstein
@sfkopstein on Unsplash

Alma Larroca
@almalarroca on Instagram

Conny Lehmann
www.aquarelle-connylehmann.com

Karen Lynch
www.leafandpetaldesign.com

Samantha Malay
http://kolajmagazine.com/artistdirectory/samantha-malay

Featured Artists *continued*

Emily Marbach
@collagenottinghill on Instagram

Julia Nala
@juliacollage on Instagram

Natalie Nelson
www.natalieknelson.com

Maddalena Notardonato
www.ritaglidalvento.com

Ciara Phelan
www.ciaraphelan.com

Argyle Plaids
@argyleplaids on Instagram

Heather Polk
www.artcuresall.com

Rosemary Rae
https://rosemaryraedesign.com

Thomas Renaud
https://lafabriquedesplis.fr

Billy Renkl
www.billyrenkl.com

Brenda Rose
www.brendarose.com

Klawe Rzeczy
@klawerzeczy on Instagram

Ginger Sedlarova
https://gingersedlarova.com

Ruby Silvious
www.rubysilvious.com

Erica K. Smith
@ericakayesmith on Instagram

Vadim Solovyev
@solovyewadim on Instagram

Gabriela Szulman
https://gabrielaszulman.com

Pamela Towns
www.pamelatowns.com

Craig Upson
@craigupson on Instagram

Ilonka van Vliet
@ilonkacollages on Instagram

Laura Weiler
www.cutandplaced.com

Erin McCluskey Wheeler
https://erinmwheeler.com

Anthony Zinonos
www.anthonyzinonos.com

Acknowledgments

I started my first ever collage-a-day challenge in December 2012 as a way to take back the Christmas season—to make it less about consumption and more about honoring the light and the quiet that exists in me and the world. Every day I made a collage and wrote something of a pep talk that I posted to my blog. This book features many of those writings, as well as my favorite ways of mixing mediums into collage.

I am forever grateful to Deborah Balmuth, whose path and history crisscrosses mine, eventually leading to the creation of this book. To Deborah, I thank you. To everyone at Storey, especially Mia Lumsden, Nancy Wood, and Liz Bevilacqua, thank you for believing in this book from the beginning and for making me a better writer. And Carolyn Eckert; your commitment to excellence should be bottled.

I am so grateful for each of the collage artists who contributed to this book. You have all touched my life and encouraged my own creativity and daily art practice in many different ways. I'm so happy to have you included in this book!

To my father, my biggest ally, who told me, "One day you will write a book," and believed in all my harebrained ideas.

To Angela Sketchpad DiGennaro, my longtime assistant. What would I do without you? Thank you for all the organizing, labeling, and collating you did to help make this book possible.

To Andrea S. D. Hazzard, one of my longest and definitely best friends ever. Your pep talks and dives into your own creative practice always inspire.

To Tara O'Brien, friend and supporter. While your honesty is sometimes hard to swallow, I know it has made me a better artist, writer, and friend. Thank you for your honest critiques!

To my early readers, Alke Groppel Wegener and Missy DelRosso, thanks for your feedback and suggestions.

To my husband, Doug, for encouraging me to work as much as I want and when I want. And for distracting me, inspiring me, and being my never-ending support and sounding board.

To Oscar the cat. Thank you for your taps of love and requests for affection. You company makes every day so much sweeter.

Index

Page numbers in *italic* indicate finished collages.

Don't think about making art, just get it done.

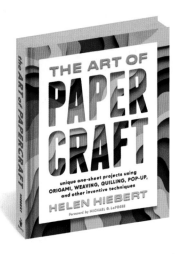